BY JAN YOORS

Crossing
The Gypsies
Only One New York

JAN YOORS

CROSSING

SIMON AND SCHUSTER · NEW YORK

FIRST PRINTING

SBN 671-20988-4
LIBRARY OF CONGRESS CATALOG CARD NUMBER: 78-156165
MANUFACTURED IN THE UNITED STATES OF AMERICA
PRINTED BY MAHONY & ROESE INC., NEW YORK, N.Y.
BOUND BY AMERICAN BOOK–STRATFORD PRESS INC., NEW YORK, N.Y.

PROLOGUE

Until the age of twelve I grew up in what seems to me, in retrospect, to have been as close to paradise as any man, or child, can wish.

My father was a painter who became a stained-glass designer. Of Flemish stock, he had grown up in the south of Spain, and his fond recollections of Andalusia pervade my own early memories like reflections of the Garden of Eden itself. And of those memories the Gitanos (the Gypsies of Spain) were an integral part. As long ago as I can remember, the Gypsies were part of my world.

My father's house, with its whitewashed two-storied skylight studio on the top floor, was a happy and sunny place. I spoke Spanish with my father, French with my mother (who was of Cuban-German descent), and German with the exchange students who helped in the household. Because at that time we lived in Flanders, I learned Flemish attending a Flemish school. Thus I learned to speak and think in four languages with equal facility, though I retained a slight foreign accent in all of them.

My father was always at home working in his huge studio where he created scale drawings of heroic size for church windows. He had a way of making his colors sing—flaming sunlike oranges, royal purples, luminous yellows, intense cobalt blues. I was allowed fairly free access to charcoals and paints and the use of a corner in his studio. There I sat for hours, drawing, painting, and dreaming. To reward my silence, good behavior, and creative output my father would tell me stories from Greek mythology, the Ramayana, and the Kalevala. Though different in nature, my relationship with my mother was equally close and happy.

When I was about twelve, Gypsies set up overnight camp on the outskirts of our town. I had an opportunity to see them at close range and in real life. The encampment consisted of about fifteen covered wagons sprawled in a wide irregular-shaped semicircle partly screening from view the activities of the camp dwellers. An occasional thin corkscrew of smoke rose to the sky. There was a profusion of half-wild dogs running about barking and howling, matched only by the number of small children, half naked or in unbelievable rags, roaming happy and free. There was sharp contrast between the static, hulking Gypsy wagons and the restless, hurried motions of children playing or throwing sticks for the dogs. In the background was the slow motion rhythm of grazing horses; in the foreground the majestic stillness of the Gypsies themselves, crouching, squatting or reclining, monumentally draped, and moving—when they did so—with deliberately slow sweeping gestures.

They were different from the Gypsies of my father's memories, who were ethereal, mythical, and above all imaginary. Even at first sight these people were earthy and my immediate impression was one of health and vitality, of exuberant animal magnetism and primitive dignity.

That day I discovered a new reality, an extended reality which I was anxious to touch, to contact before it disappeared, before the Gypsies mysteriously vanished again leaving nothing more than wagon tracks in the soft ground, trampled grass, and a few dark spots where the campfires had burned.

As I stepped resolutely through tall weeds toward the camp, none of the adults appeared to heed my intrusion but several boys my age ran to meet me. As sometimes happens between very young human beings, there was from the beginning a feeling of great ease, almost one of having met before. During that afternoon of the late spring in the mid-1930s we became friends—inseparable friends, as circumstances developed. There were Nanosh, Laetshi, Putzina, and several others. They shared with me their interests and vital concerns, first by showing me the horses of the tribe. They taught me what they considered to be the basic division between the Rom (themselves) and the Gaje (all non-Gypsies). From the slight hesitation in Nanosh's voice I divined the pejorative connotation they attached to the word, revealing to my naïve surprise that the Rom might have as many prejudices against us, the Gaje, as we had against them.

That night I stayed on. I ate with them and sat by the blazing campfire and listened fascinated to the Gypsies singing and talking. I accepted Nanosh's invitation to share, together with his many little brothers, his sleeping stead between two huge eiderdowns laid out under the starry sky. Unintended and unplanned as that first night away from home had been, it was repeated again and again so that I did not know how to break away and return home. As long as the summer holiday weather lasted, I did not, perhaps, try overly hard to return, even though I remained aware of the anomaly of my situation and knew my parents were waiting for me and must have been worried. Yet I stayed away six months. I became separated from my first young Gypsy friend, Nanosh, but was adopted by Putzina and his father Pulika. In time, and for all practical purposes, I became fully assimilated into their entire family.

I eventually returned to my parents, who with great love and rare insight coped with my youthful dilemma, which enabled me to deal with it myself.

After the dreary winter months spent in the comfort and safety of my parents' home, with the only partially satisfying challenge of school, I resumed my wanderings with the Gypsies. This time, however, with my parents' knowledge and, if not their approval or encouragement, at least with their tacit consent. They imposed one single condition: if I became involved in any complications or trouble I would turn to them first for advice and assistance. This was a marked contrast to the more conventional advice: "Don't come back to us when you are in trouble."

After spending many months with the Gypsies, spellbound and intensely happy, one day I would suddenly feel an impelling eagerness to go back to my parents and the world of the

Gaje. I left the Gypsies as impulsively and as unpredictably as I had left my parents in the first place. It was like waking from a strange, wondrous dream.

My homecoming was always a joyous event. In Antwerp, the house with the large skylight studio was sunny, comfortable, happy, and permeated with the familiar smells of beeswax and freshly baked bread and cakes. Everywhere there were books, paintings, Oriental rugs, and classical music. Returning to my parents' home I wondered what it was that made me willing to live all those months with the Gypsies, without the comfort and ease I had been brought up to consider normal, desirable, even indispensable. I made a feast of the rediscovered luxury of a hot bath, clean clothes, and a good haircut. In contrast, I would at unexpected moments wonder how young Kore or Nanosh would react to all the physical comforts of my present life. Simultaneously, the world of covered wagons and tents, of the dark-skinned people who were my exuberant, joyous, barefoot companions not long ago seemed far away. Even the thought of them made me smile. It all seemed as totally unreal, but as distinctly desirable, as a strange half-forgotten dream.

I applied myself to school studies and tried hard by my good behavior to make up for my earlier unaccountable lapse in running away with the Gypsies, and that interlude receded into an unbelievable past. Then one day at lunchtime my father casually mentioned that a band of nomads was camping on the outskirts of town. What I secretly feared most happened again: I was faced with a decision for which I still felt unprepared. I was drawn to the Gypsies as by a magnet and felt strangely unable to shake off their spell. Again I joined them, sleeping under the open sky, alternately eating meager fare and overabundant feasts. Again I was part of the dream of all normal, healthy boys in a well-organized, established society—to participate in the hard adventurous life of pioneers and early settlers, the kind of life which challenged boys to become men.

My first two stays with the Rom stand out clearly in my memory as times of wonder and discovery. I also distinctly remember my first homecoming, my anxious, guilty anticipation and the shock of relief when it happened. After this the alternating periods with the Rom and at my parents' home fuse into one. On the surface I lived two separate but intertwined lives, true and intense in each even though they seemed poles apart. After each winter-long separation from them, I had to pick up the erratic trail of my Gypsy family so that, looking back, I wonder at my persistent luck. Sometimes it happened that Pulika and his band had traveled far away, crossing several national borders. Occasionally this made my joining the Rom again something of a minor spy hunt, following elusive indications, or even mere guesses, and illegally crossing frontiers with the help of other Rom. More than any other, this particular aspect of my life with the Rom seems even today a chain of improbabilities, yet undeniably real.

At home my parents rarely spoke about the Gypsies, certainly never against them. The Rom remained my very own private, secret domain. Because of the Gypsies' doubtful social status and my circumvention of the laws about obligatory education, very few people were aware of my double life. When I returned to school after a prolonged, but strictly pretended, convalescence, my healthy suntan and overflow of energy were difficult to explain away. Because I could not tell about the Gypsies so dear to me and influential to my development, I told instead about my life among the "Redskins." Few people ever suspected that the adventures I related in glowing terms, and no doubt with convincing accuracy, really had happened to me.

As each year passed I became more a Gypsy and less a Gajo, though in grateful appreciation of my parents' trust in me I faithfully visited them every year in Antwerp and later on in London. I was torn between two worlds and unable to choose.

In 1939, after the great annual fall meeting of the *Romani kris* (the law court and tribal council of the Rom) they had seemed more reluctant than usual to disperse. There had been extravagant celebrations of friendship and they lingered on, endlessly reciprocating one another's hospitality. Even when the extraordinary ingathering of the Rom suddenly dissolved, they broke camp in the anarchistic way of the Gypsies and scattered in all directions. Large numbers of wagons converged again a few miles farther along. Many of the Rom traveled together while remaining in the same general area. And the feasting went on. The celebrations were hardly interrupted by the daily need and obligation to move camp; singing and drinking continued even when the Rom were actually on the road. It was the period of harvest and in their own right the peasants were in an equally expansive mood.

Like the gentle but obsessive rustling of the cornfields, the dominant theme of conversation had turned to matchmaking and marriages. The unusually large gathering of the Rom offered a wide choice of possible matches, and the desire to prolong the prevailing festive mood contributed further to finding valid excuses for this. Among themselves the Rom appraised the girls (whose parents they might approach on the behalf of their sons) in a direct, realistic, but never disrespectful manner. In Romanes the word "girl," *shei,* also meant a virgin, which the Rom expected them to be. The Lowara* believed that an unchaste woman knowingly tolerated in their midst brought dissent and eventually bad luck, and because of the rather strict sexual mores of their people there was a nearly total absence of premarital experimentation or flirta-

---

* The Lowara (singular Lowari) are members of an important tribe of purely nomadic Gypsies who wander over the entire world, from Chile to Siberia, from Finland to South Africa and Australia. There is a basic distinction between the sedentary and the nomadic Gypsies—who originated in northwestern India and came to Europe via Afghanistan in staggered waves of immigration beginning roughly in the fourteenth century—which has seldom been clearly brought out. In the popular mind, Gypsy has come to mean nomadic. In fact, a large number of Gypsies have voluntarily (or otherwise) settled in specific areas, like the Gitanos in Spain, the Tchinghianes in Turkey, the Erlides in Bulgaria, the Rudarits of Rumania, and many others in the Balkans and elsewhere. Their language, customs, and religion have become strongly influenced by those of their "host countries"; in view of this they are often identified as Spanish Gypsies, Turkish Gypsies, Greek Gypsies, Hungarian Gypsies, in contrast to the purely nomadic Gypsies, the Rom.

tion. The Lowara said that a man should select his future daughter-in-law "with the ears and not with the eyes," meaning that more consideration should be given to a girl's reputation than to her beauty. The assembled men sagaciously speculated about each girl's potential as a future wife.

A substantial bridal price was paid in gold pieces and the traditional bargaining session (which, even between close friends, had nonetheless a mock solemnity) was elaborate and longdrawn. It was, in fact and for all practical purposes, the true marriage ceremony. It was crowned, or sealed, by all parties concerned drinking from the *pliashka* (brandy bottle) hung with gold pieces. Later, on another day, came the banquet and the groom's ceremonial abduction of the bride with the assistance of his bachelor male relatives. The morning after saw a ritual, but genuine, display of the bridal linen as proof of her prior virginity, and the symbolic rebraiding of the bride's hair and knotting of the kerchief covering her head as sign of the woman who belongs, the married woman. Newlyweds remained with the groom's parents, at least until the birth of the first or the second child.

The camp was endlessly busy, for not one but several marriages were in the making. Various delegations of important Rom who acted as matchmakers or go-betweens had visited the parents of at least four different girls. It was not yet disclosed on whose behalf requests were made.

Until my adopted older sister Keja rebuffed me crossly for letting Pulika arrange a marriage for me, it had not occurred to me that one of the marriages being planned might be my own. Keja, who had earlier stood aloof, abruptly said that by temperamental disposition I was not meant to live with the Lowara, that among them I would never find ultimate fulfillment. This hit me like a cloudburst. Keja was the person with whom I felt the most affinity. I admired her strength and her spirit, her self-reliance and her resourcefulness. Nothing had prepared me for her clear, uncompromising, total rejection. She went on to say that I was cowardly in not taking a stand against marriage, that I was about to make a serious mistake, for inevitably I would leave. There would be children, my children, and it could only mean my wife's ruin. I myself, she was sure, would not be able to forget, to fully wipe away, what had been; or I might stand by my choice, stay with the Lowara and my wife, and waste my life and potential. I wanted to protest my love and loyalty, yet in an uncanny way I knew she was right.

I boldly sought out Pulika near the grazing horses in the pastures and blurted out to him what troubled me, only to have him dissipate my anguish with a conciliatory embrace. For a while we smoked in silence before walking back to the camp. Overhead in the deep blue sky a flight of wild geese in arrowhead formation headed south on their seasonal migration. They honked excitedly. Years before, when I had first joined the Gypsies, Pulika's wife Rupa had called me a "wild goose," *vadni ratsa,* because of my sudden absences. At that time it struck me as unexpected that a Gypsy could allude to my wanderlust and unpredictability when in fact it was the Gypsies themselves who exemplified for me these attributes of a bird of passage.

I refused flight as the solution, but I knew that staying on with the Rom was no solution either; the conflict of dual loyalty would recur soon enough. Prompted by Keja's perceptive and loyal affection, I faced the moment of truth, admitting to myself my unwillingness to accept total, unqualified absorption in the world of the Lowara by marrying the girl Pulika had chosen to be mine. I had unwittingly crossed the threshold of manhood, but in a manner Pulika could not have anticipated. A serene melancholy replaced the disquiet and uncertainty. For the Rom, the only form of initiation into the world of the men was marriage. Theirs was a cult of the family and the feminine ideal was that of the mother. Celibacy was unthinkable and unnatural. I was concerned about the implications of my rejection of Djidjo as a wife—she fulfilled in my eyes all imaginable prerequisites of an ideal bride, Gypsy or other—yet under the particular circumstances and at this particular time I was almost equally concerned about the implications of my rejection of marriage itself.

I appreciated the fact that in somehow conveying my unsus-

pected unwillingness to marry the daughter of Dodo la Kejako
—it was, admittedly, at the eleventh hour that I was made
aware of the inadequacy of my love and loyalty to the Rom—
Pulika had to try to save her reputation and her father's
honor. Contrary to the tradition of the Lowara, Pulika had,
considerately and lovingly, allowed his choice for a future
daughter-in-law and mate for me to be guided by my personal
attention to and yearning for Djidjo—something which obviously had not escaped his attention.

The first time I became aware of Djidjo and her sister Ludu
had been a few months earlier at a roadside encampment
somewhere in Voivodina. Pulika and his *kumpania* had joined
Dodo la Kejako after illegally crossing the border under the
cover of night. Our host had two nubile daughters and I remember being disturbed by their youthful grace, not yet
awakened to full womanhood. Their long black hair was in a
single braid and they had a mysteriously disarming combination of innocence and sensuousness. My brother Kore had to
sharply remind me of Lowara propriety before I could take
my eyes off them. The youngest, Djidjo, was a strange, skittish
child-woman. She sang in the rain, feared the moon, and was
haunted by night clouds. Once I saw her singing in the pouring rain. The water streamed down her face and neck to
disappear between her breasts, slightly darkening her skin.
Her voice was soft, sweet, and low. She was said to be wild
and ungovernable. Many months later, when an opportunity
presented itself, Pulika had formally approached her father.
And now all this was over. I was relieved to find out how
unobtrusively the matter had been solved. Yojo started an
argument which led to the marriage being postponed on the
objection of an infraction of Romani tradition: Kore and
Keja, both older than I, were still unmarried. And besides,
Djidjo's older sister Ludu was still a virgin.

Shortly after this Pulika sent me away with several other
Rom and their wives, ostensibly to visit the Kalderasha tribes-
men who lived on the outskirts of Paris. They were nomadic
coppersmiths who had originally come out of Russia. After a
short absence I joined Pulika's *kumpania* again. I was made to

feel welcome, loved, and in many ways spoiled. Yet I could not help feeling that an irremediable parting of ways had taken place. One day I happened to cross Djidjo's path on her way to the river to fetch water. She, the little wild one, unaware yet of my deepening estrangement from the Rom, was awkward in her emotion and I sensed in her a tenderness I had not suspected. Her hips swayed gently and she threw back an unruly forelock, but she had already displayed to me a willing quietness that implied the promise of eventual marital obedience.

The die was cast, but I could not help wonder fleetingly if my renunciation of her was not an excess of discretion. It made only more enticing and desirable the well-rounded slender figure undulating under the loose, full, yet revealing garment. In the fall of 1939 I had reached the point of no return.

PART ONE

CHAPTER ONE

The tenth of May, 1940, was sunny and bright. It was the beginning of the angry years which were to engulf the Gypsies and the world. In my half-slumber I heard a faint purr overhead in the paling night sky. The not unpleasant noise grew ominous and as I fully awakened I saw wave upon wave of planes pass over us. One by one they tipped their wings and seemed to fall, releasing their bombs.

The large wagon camp of the Gypsies lay sprawled in an idyllic wooded hollow on the Belgian side of the French border, surrounded by a great expanse of lush meadows. The night had been pleasantly warm and we had slept under the sky. Some of the ashes of the woodfires, studding the encampment with dark spots, were still warm. The numerous horses massed about us panicked as the slow flight of bombers fell in a high-pitched screaming, followed shortly after by the rumble of distant thunder. We saw black columns of billowing smoke and heard sirens wail like wounded animals. The drone of the airplanes again grew faint, ending in a faraway rustle. Nature became oppressively silent.

Terrified and fascinated we had watched the bombing. After having been momentarily possessed, we were now equally astonished to be still alive. Most of the Gypsies had still been sleeping under their featherbeds. They hastily dressed themselves under the bedcovers and the colorful eiderdowns shook and moved convulsively. The small children scrambled out into the open stark naked: the older ones seeking shelter beneath the massive wagons, the small ones nestling themselves close to their parents as they would have done during a thunderstorm. Some of the women wailed and shrieked as if they had lost their minds, ripped their clothes as if in the grip of a holy terror, and rocked themselves back and forth violently, or rolled their heads madly sideways, as they did during funerals. The violence of their distress shook me out of my frozen stupor. Among the crouched, prostrated, and huddled figures of the Rom, ancient Lyuba stood alone and erect. She had a wild expression in her unblinking eyes, reflecting both amazement and scorn as she stared at the distant sky. Her arms were outstretched. One fist closed in menace while the fingers of the other hand opened and closed rhythmically, symbolically grasping the offenders—the retreating Luftwaffe bomber planes, by now tiny specks high up and far away. The Rom's extreme reaction, at once frenzied, terrified, and exultant, was not unlike their behavior at a wake, exorcising the immediate paralysis of grief. A wild clamor arose from the camp in an intense outburst of collective, almost orgiastic, madness, with the violent, extravagant abandon of the Rom.

Old Lyuba, fierce and scowling still, was the first to regain her composure. She walked back slowly and crouched by the glowing embers of the fire she had lit for herself, apart from the fires of the families of her children and grandchildren, well before anybody else in the camp had awakened. After the first violent explosion of savage frenzy, the Rom brewed their strong, black, sweet coffee.

Dika, old Butsulo's sickly wife, yelled, "The end of the world has come. Let us run away before more bombs fall on us." Rupa called after her, *"I tshirikleski kul tshi perel duvar pe yek than"*—the droppings of the [flying] bird never fall twice on the same spot.

When the men realized that no immediate danger threatened their families and their camp, they ran to the pastures, followed by the younger boys, to catch the panicked horses and bring them under control. The herd of horses, running in close formation, wheeled around and stampeded away in terror in a different direction. The men worked in unison. They waved their arms wildly and uttered wild, high-pitched sounds and wolflike whistles. Gradually they broke up the herd and cornered a few horses, leaving the wilder, more recalcitrant and frightened ones. The isolated horses bared their teeth and reared, while others nervously turned sideways and kicked. The men now made deep rumbling sounds, meant to reassure and appease the animals, and they moved with deliberately slow and controlled movements. The Rom were experienced with horses and there were no mishaps. After having subdued the horses, the Rom mounted and led them back to the camp through vast expanses of spongy grasslands. The horses were frisky and spattered a hail of mud as they went. Pulika's stallion gave Kore particular trouble; he hung on to the halter with all his weight to bend its neck and prevent its rearing out of control.

The Rom rode into the camp and tied their horses to the rear of the wagons, keeping them near at hand in case they had to break camp in a hurry. The boys rubbed the horses down, currycombed and calmed them. By now many cooking fires had been lit. The women had peeled onions and potatoes and fried meat with tomatoes, pepper, and garlic were stewing in black castiron pots. Breakfast was ready. Dark-skinned young women with milk-swollen breasts nursed their babies, squatting or walking about doing chores. The camp had recovered its normal rhythm.

The sun was hot and the earth smelled good. From every direction distant churchbells incessantly tolled the beginning of war.

Unthinking, panic-stricken, the entire population fled from the deluge, away from the advancing German legions surging forward. All roads leading south and southwest were clogged with trucks, buses, bicycles, private cars, pushcarts, and wheelbarrows piled high with blankets, mattresses, pots, pans, suitcases, and other household articles. Some fled on foot; others were without luggage. Strategic arteries, which had been forbidden to civilians, were now massively and systematically dive-bombed by the German Stukas, disrupting all effective military action.

Wherever the swelling mass of refugees surged they contaminated others with the same unreasoning panic. Everywhere the leaders, civilian as well as military, had already been evacuated "farther south," abusing the responsibility of their rank to procure themselves transportation. In the prevailing chaos some summarily commandeered civilian cars (as a last resort, to be sure), leaving the owners and their passengers stranded. The lesser functionaries often tried heroically to stem the tide before they themselves were wrenched loose and in turn were swept away in the infectious terror of total anarchy.

The National Guard, the Gendarmerie, and the administrative cadres were completely swamped and bypassed by the unforeseen speed and scale of what was happening. Churches, schools, parochial halls and town halls were used as emergency shelters. The inordinate number of refugees kept growing until even these shelters had to be restricted to the infirm, the sick, small children, and pregnant women. Here too, hopeless chaos arose and all semblance of order broke down. In the early days of this exodus certain communities along its route provided hot soup, coffee, or cocoa for the transients. A few army mobile kitchens which had been separated from their units helped feed the hungry while their supplies lasted.

Profiteers and exploiters sold food at outrageous prices to the equally immoral highest bidders, "as the marketplace set the price." With callous rapacity, not a few local inhabitants charged money for a glass of cold water. Many refugees were reduced to drinking ditchwater. The humble or the less affluent would go thirsty for many miles in the burning sun until they reached a public pump. The frenzied mob trudged on day and night, uncontrollable, lost to all reason.

German fighter planes swooped down from the clear skies and flew low over the crowded roads to indiscriminately machine-gun the fleeing populace, leaving trucks burning and people dying, women and children hysterical. Those who had managed to scramble off the road and into the nearby fields scrambled back onto the road more determined and more desperate than before to push on. People who had lived in ease, comfort, and safety were reduced overnight to harsh privations, exposed to the elements as in a shipwreck or a natural disaster.

In the countryside, through the fields bordering the roads, were manhunts and lynchings (probably of innocents) as frustration bred violence and homicidal hysteria spread. Once the full shock of impending defeat set in, there was an inarticulate, eroding sense of betrayal and ominous anticipation of the agonies to come. The exodus grew.

The Rom had had little choice but to join the others. Day after day the bombing continued. Night skies were red and the reek of burning never left us. Bridges were down, telephones dead, and all other communications disrupted. After the first few days the roadsides were lined with private cars and trucks, abandoned because of malfunction or for lack of gasoline, still laden with belongings. I remember seeing a hearse, old-fashioned, lugubrious, ornate, all black-and-gold, that had been used for escape; when it became useless it had been overturned into a ditch to clear the road. Everywhere were suitcases, chairs, and mattresses, jettisoned as the fleeing population grew more tired and increasingly concerned with saving lives rather than property, though a few pathetic exceptions elected to collapse of exhaustion rather than abandon what was theirs.

A small covey of heavily made-up prostitutes clumsily tried to cover their garish dresses with plebeian shawls. Their provocatively corseted figures seemed out of place in the harsh light of day. A group of young men on bicycles, mobilized but not yet in uniform and unencumbered by personal luggage, passed by on their way to induction centers farther south, "somewhere in France." Depending on the density of traffic or on sudden obstructions, they changed their formation, cycling several abreast or in single file, weaving, passing, fluttering with one foot on tiptoe to the ground to maintain balance, pushing themselves forward, and pedaling furiously whenever a stretch of road permitted.

In austere little uniforms, a flock of orphans followed in close formation, hemmed in by concerned-looking nuns. Their drawn white faces, like slight, paltry moons, floated against and seemed dissociated from the voluminous black habits of their order. Earlier we had observed an incredible procession of distressing inmates from an insane asylum. Most of the men were subdued, totally alienated, their eyes hooded by incomprehension, bereft of reason. A few were dejected, oblivious to everything. Others were incoherent, simple-minded, babbling inconsequentially. Still others appeared to be under considerable strain, frenzied, and these were closely guarded by burly attendants in white smocks. Looking at them, I wondered briefly what would be the lot of inmates confined to prisons or other penitentiary institutions. I wondered about all those in emergency wards of hospitals, the terminal cases, and those attending them. I thought—and I distinctly remember the disturbing impression about the seeming incongruity and triviality—about the fate of animals in the zoos. By association this brought me to Noah and his ark facing the deluge, attempting to obey God's commandment to save "every living thing of all flesh, two of every sort shalt thou bring into the ark, to keep them alive with thee. . . ."

The masses fled and endured. After many days on the roads conditions gradually worsened. Fear, hunger, thirst, and lack of sleep accumulated. Most slept on straw, many simply on the ground. Only the most privileged managed to obtain more conventional lodgings. Many people considered themselves entitled to more proper facilities and, like spoiled children, bitterly demanded the impossible. The marchers suffered painful sunburns. Nobody had foreseen the need for suntan lotions and few were used to constant exposure. Their feet were badly blistered for lack of proper walking shoes. Many had become infested by vermin and no disinfectants were to be had. They were plagued by colics and digestive disorders. Their eyes burned with fever and lack of sleep. They were uprooted and homesick and they knew there was no way to turn back. Conventional class distinctions, social importance, economic status, all were obliterated.

Lost among the interminable crowds were small contingents of anxious Jewish refugees with their own special sense of urgency. Among these were pious Jews in long black caftans and black hats, with unkempt beards, flowing sidelocks, and pale faces. They clung together and moved with rapid awkward strides, displaying an intense nervous energy which belied their unathletic appearance. They seemed to cling to their *Yiddishkeit,* their Jewishness, and to find consolation in it.

Mischief-makers of all kinds, crooks, pimps, and cutthroats were wrenched loose from their habitual niches to mingle with the crowds. Often they were among the first to regain their composure and revert to their previous ways, to take advantage of opportunity and of the innocents. Because of the lack of transportation, pilfering from deserted houses along the road was mostly limited to "appropriating" food or medical supplies, socks, blankets, pillows, or bicycles which, inconceivable as it may seem, had been left behind. Unconsciously crystallizing the general loss of meaning and reference, young vandals wreaked wanton destruction. They invaded homes, ripped and slashed curtains, threw disemboweled mattresses out of windows, turned on upstairs water faucets to watch the overflow cascade down the stairs. They defecated everywhere as a curious but conspicuous symbol of their defiance.

In contrast to the colorless haggard mass of fleeing city people, desperate, gray-skinned, ill-washed, uncombed, disheveled, unshaven, tired, and hungry, the Gypsies stood out sharply. Like the flowers of the fields they wore a colorful array of magentas, blues, oranges, and deep yellows which brought out their exuberant health and vitality, their dark skin and jet-black hair, their clear eyes, strong teeth, and sturdy good looks. Shaped by the exigencies of their nomadic existence, the Rom had evolved a way of life attuned to emergencies. Their sense of survival was better honed. They moved with a clearer sense of purpose, with greater dignity. Their material possessions were whittled down to the absolute minimum and geared effectively toward survival. Yet the Gypsies' voluntary, if extreme, penury of material possessions was amply compensated by their enviable sense of relatedness, the intimacy they felt among their own kind, their awareness of being part of a larger whole. Unbothered by preoccupations with the past or the future, they were content to live in an

everlasting, self-renewing, heroic present. They chose to glo-
rify the encounters with their own, to vie with each other in
demonstrations of generosity. Their ethic was cooperative
rather than competitive. The Rom had elaborated ingenious
ways to protect their identity and cultural continuity. These
could range from their display of poverty (albeit most often
feigned) to their projected aura of magic, the supernatural,
and fortune-telling. In this way they excluded and screened
out by invisible walls the implacable and often hostile outside
world much as the Gaje erected walls to keep out the disturbing element of nature. "Inside," in the privacy of their exclusive domain, there existed a reality often the exact opposite of
the appearance shown "outside." Here they could afford to
indulge in a rare capacity for affection, tenderness, trust,
concern, and respect. In contrast to the Gaje, who could
always watch the Gypsies live, the private lives of the non-
Gypsies had been screened from the Rom, who in their turn
could now observe the others live. The Rom wondered at the
incomprehensible attachment the Gaje had for things. They
were amused by their need to possess. Until then the Rom had
dismissed the Gaje as unworthy of interest. Now the Rom
lived in close proximity to them. But novelty soon wore off.
Rupa scornfully called them "sleepwalkers." She said, "To
understand the Gaje, like the blind, you must close your eyes."

The Rom, having survived the first shock of war, were now
as gay as birds after the rain, continuing to live as they always
had. They traveled every day, but now they were carried on
the tide of refugees. They knew how to select well-suited
campsites near flowing water or in the shade of trees, and their
high-wheeled wagons easily pulled off the roads and onto
rough terrain. They made short raiding forays off the main
roads and never failed to bring back abundant provisions:
chicken, geese, and pigs. The Rom lived a way of life in which
the necessity to kill in order to eat had not yet been forgotten.
They were dismayed to see how easily large numbers of Gaje
lost their heads and succumbed to despair under adverse
circumstances.

Dark, wild, unkempt little Boti, barely ten years old and

who already dabbled in fortune-telling, remarked in mock sympathy, "The Gaje constantly wish that things were different. In summer they want snow and in winter sunshine. Don't they realize that you cannot buy what is not for sale?" To which Keja added with finality, *"O ushalin jala sar o kam mangela"*—the shadow moves as the sun commands.

The orchards along the dusty roads leading south were blossoming and the potato beetles had started on their rampage. One day we reached the river Somme in Picardy, somewhere between Abbeville and Amiens in the north of France, only to find most of the bridges had been destroyed by the retreating French and British troops. Before we had time to find a ford, a pontoon, or any other means to cross we were caught by an advancing German tank column.

Following Pulika's lead the other covered wagons of our group swung off the main road—partly to clear the way for enemy tanks roaring by—onto a deeply grooved dirt track through weed-infested fields of sugar beets and into the partial seclusion of a farmyard. It was a fairly large farmstead, deserted and half collapsed as so many in that region seemed to be. We were greeted by scattering chickens and honking geese. A number of men of various nationalities, all of military draft age, had preceded us and were already encamped in the large haylofts. The Rom took over several large outbuildings. They drove the wagons inside and kept the horses out of sight. Fires were lit inside the buildings and the women discreetly went foraging for edibles. We joined some of the Polish coalminers and farmhands who gathered in the main part of the farmhouse to listen to a radio. They explained, in case we were not aware of this, that earlier on their country had been attacked, conquered, and divided between the Nazis and the Soviets. They themselves were recent expatriates who had sought employment in northern France. As a group they seethed with hatred for the Germans and had a passionate determination to fight to the end. The few sulking French citizens holed up on neighboring farms glowered at us, implying our complicity with the enemy, in a vain attempt to alleviate their own sense of inadequacy, humiliation, and guilt by making others the scapegoats. Were we not, after all, dirty foreigners?

The Germans had imposed a strict curfew and all civilian circulation was prohibited in the fighting zone. For several days we rested there, undisturbed except for false alarms, an armored personnel carrier snarling by, occasional shellings, or airplane fights overhead. In the distance we could hear the Germans singing in unison as they paraded in their black or *feldgrau* uniforms. Their singing sounded beautiful, but their goosestepping aroused only disbelief, derision, and wonder. Another day three tanks came roaring up ominously in the afternoon heat, leaving behind a trail of dust. Their turrets moved around in a searching sweep of the surroundings. The turret cupolas were open and healthy, smiling, adolescent soldiers with light blue eyes in sunburned sweating faces leaned out and waved at us. This was our first direct contact with our conquerors.

When the heavy artillery from across the Somme stopped booming, the endless convoys of German armored troop carriers and war matériel resumed the advance. The civilian population had not been unduly molested. In view of the hysterical Germanophobic heritage of the war of 1914–18 and because of the prevailing parachutist psychosis, people had anticipated a worse fate and were relieved that it was all over so soon and so easily.

Paris fell and the victorious Germans halted their advance, leaving part of France unoccupied. An armistice was signed.

The stringent curfew of the first few days of the invasion was lifted. After this period of forced rest the Polish contingent made ready to proceed on its journey south. They planned to make their way first to the unoccupied zone of France and from there to North Africa to join the Foreign Legion, if they fought on. If not they would proceed to England and, if England fell, they would go on to America to fight.

One of the Gypsies in our group (Punka, I believe) spoke Polish and had made contact with them. They talked late into the night after one of the sessions around the wireless set listening to the French-language news from London. As the Poles left the farmyard they bantered with Punka, yet there was a peculiar sting to their words even in their obvious intent at camaraderie, an echo of implied violence stemming from generations of ethnic discrimination. Most of the refugees set out for home, although men of military draft age remained out of sight of the Germans for some time to come for fear of being deported as prisoners of war.

Of necessity, formal relations with the enemy gradually evolved and soon became routine. Because of severe food shortages, an emergency system of rationing was instituted. The black-out, which at least in theory had been imposed since the Franco-British declaration of war on Germany but which had been little observed, was now stringently enforced by the Germans. Long before the Blitzkrieg, the French government had arrested and detained as undesirable aliens many political refugees from Germany and many from countries occupied by the Nazis. They had arrested and detained the defeated Spanish Loyalists who had fled to France, as well as all those who sided with them. Their antifascist political loyalties were well known. Many Gypsies were arrested under the cloak of this same national security measure and were interned in such camps as Le Vernet, Linas-Monthléry, Seine-et-Oise, Rennes, Mulhouse, and Sarthe. After the surrender of France, these captives were in many cases summarily handed over to the Gestapo for "processing" and transported to Germany's eastern front. Like the Jews, the Gypsies were declared enemies of the Reich, *Rassenverfolgte,* and as such were legislated out of existence. Posters appeared announcing the edicts of the conquerors. All weapons in the possession of civilians were to be surrendered promptly under penalty of death; sheltering enemy agents, enemy aviators, or escaped prisoners of war, or failing to report such activities by others, was to be punished by death. It was *verboten* to listen to radio broadcasts by the "enemy," which meant the British and all such governments and Free French Forces fighting for national survival and honor beside them. It was *verboten* to circulate without an

Ausweis, or special permit, from the German Kommandant. All long-distance transportation was under German control. There were forms to fill, checkpoints, roadblocks. *Verboten* became part of the new vocabulary. Restrictions were imposed on fishing vessels off North Sea shores. The property of those who had escaped to England was confiscated. Requisitions of basic products began. Traitors to the national cause and collaborators with the occupiers sprang up everywhere. Blacklists were circulated and members of the political opposition were hunted down. People whispered and learned to fear. When the mail service was restored it was with the added flourish of German censorship. Letters were opened, often whole passages deleted, and disquieting cryptic annotations added on the outside of the envelopes. There was a rash of anonymous letters of denunciation. And even though the national press (with new titles and editorial staffs) was obviously controlled, frequently there were blank spaces due to further last-minute censorship. The telephone service, sporadic at best, was often tapped. The Germans built a maze of shifting restrictions, highly varied, often arbitrary, to destroy the will and the capacity of the people to resist. Posters announced the arrest of leading citizens as hostages, many of them never to return.

After the fierce air battles over Great Britain and a clandestinely rumored attempted invasion, the Germans built an elaborate system of coastal defense along the North Sea shores after evacuating most of the local population. By "digging in," they clearly implied that the war would be longer than they had been willing to concede in their initial euphoria.

A mood of restiveness and frustration prevailed, tempered by a cautious disposition to wait and see. Impressed by the apparent futility of their plight and fearful of chaos, the vanquished were willing to obey any authority that could guarantee order. They knew they would have to live with whomever won the war.

During a brief idyllic period the Germans released numerous POWs in a gesture of calculated generosity, even though from the French contingent alone more than one and a half million men remained in captivity for the duration of the war. Soon, however, kidnappings became increasingly frequent as the repressive agencies became active. The Gestapo, the Sicherheitsdienst, the Geheime Feld Polizei, the Abwehr, and others often were in jealous competition with one another and, to the added woe of their quarries, their activities overlapped. People learned to whisper, to fear, and to anticipate the predawn knock on the door.

An initial appeal by the Germans for volunteer labor lured by profit and adventure failed dismally. Then began the wholesale deportation of skilled labor for compulsory work in Germany's war industry, according to a deportation priority structure on a stand-by basis—thus proving a long and thorough preparation. Everybody had been forced to register, after which, like a film frozen on a single frame, no one was permitted to change either his employment or his residence. Certain categories benefited from preferential treatment out of absolute necessity, as minimal cadres were needed to keep the country functioning. Among these were included employees of the postal services, police, garbage disposal, water and electrical power, public transportation, and various key administrative services, all those indispensable to maintain production in agriculture, mines, and the steel industry. Misbehavior, or the simple accusation of misbehaving, was punished by prompt deportation.

A new spirit of brutality prevailed as the enemy finally revealed his character. There followed the marked increase and intensification of manhunts and police raids. Recalcitrant elements were quickly singled out and ruthlessly eliminated for the sake of setting examples. Yet against the slow tide of anguish people hoped against hope and clung desperately to a dumb unwillingness to admit that things had changed. Despair set in and eroded the will to live.

It became a common sight to see handcuffed prisoners marched off between German soldiers in their impeccable uniforms and their high boots. Jews, often longtime and respected residents of the particular country in which they had become almost totally assimilated, were dragged away from their residences to be herded together in squalid ghettos. Many of these people were indistinguishable from any other citizen, except by careful scrutiny of their genealogies, while others were only recently escaped refugees from German-occupied eastern Europe. These people looked particularly outlandish in their long, shiny carefully tailored black caftans and their fur hats, their *shtreimels,* like the ones we had seen on the roads of France during the Blitzkrieg. They had wild untrimmed beards, sidelocks, tired red eyes; as they were marched away they covered their heads with their long fringed prayer shawls. They sang softly or said prayers, sobbing. The women and children, dressed in an old-fashioned manner with long white stockings, were haggard and silent. A shockingly contrapuntal surrealistic element one could never invent was a group of Hassidim, swaying wildly back and forth in the sacred rhythm of religious ecstasy, as if participating in an incomprehensible, inconceivable frenzy of religious joy.

In the conquered territory the Jews were gradually hemmed in, isolated, herded together, and moved about in what seemed to be meaningless numbing exercises. Bit by bit they were stripped of their ability to resist. There were reports of unexplained last-minute reprieves. Exemptions were said to have been made for Jews of certain "privileged" nationalities. Others were rumored to have been released for a ransom. Illusory systems of privilege were encouraged to prevent unity and resistance.

Against this somber background the Gypsies lived as they always had. Pulika and the Rom knew, and their knowledge was confirmed almost daily and by endless undefinable indications, that they too were marked for vengeance, that they would soon be brutally rounded up. For them the time would also come to be nothing more than hunted beasts, to be destroyed "for the benefit of Mankind," as had already those Gypsies caught within the expanding boundaries of the Reich. All along the Rom had not been deluded. Many had felt the urge to go west to the Americas; but whereas they were adept at crossing borders by illegal methods, being illiterate and lacking adequate documents, they were at a disadvantage in negotiating the more complex administrative paperwork necessary to obtain immigration visas. Belatedly I learned that Pulika had tried on the behalf of his *kumpania* and failed. Now it was too late; the Rom were caught. They knew there was to be no mercy, or, as they said, you must not expect mercy from the merciless.

From the beginning of the Nazi takeover of Germany, the Gypsies, like the Jews, were singled out and discriminated against as *Artfremdes Blut,* alien blood, and as such were merely a problem to be solved. Men like Kommandant Hans Globke of the Nürnberger Rassengesetzgebung, Rassenlehrer Hans Guenther, Robert Koerber, and the Gypsy expert Professor Robert Ritter* devoted their attention to the problem. The RSHA sent out directives to the Kripo, or Criminal Police, concerning the repression against Gypsy "nonpersons," in the name of crime prevention, as distinguished from purely racial considerations. Many Gypsies were arrested, some as early as 1936, as *arbeitsscheue und asoziale* (labor-shy and asocial) and sent to Dachau and Ravensbrueck.

At the same time the Gypsies were declared *Freiwild,* their extermination was left to the individual responsibility and discretion of the local SS Führer. This administrative practice led to mass executions by SS Erschiessungspelotons, as well as by the various Ukrainian, Polish, or Croat fascists.

In Germany the repression started with compulsory settlement and a ban on unauthorized traveling; then came special identity cards, registration and investigation by a new office, the Zigeunerdezernat, where the Gypsies were "evaluated" according to a complex system of racial classification through which they were divided into pure, less pure, and impure categories. Special camps were organized for the Gypsies of Germany and Austria: the *Zigeunersammelplatze* in Lackenbach, Bruckhaufen, near Vienna, Leopoldskron, near Salzburg, Hopfgarten. After the invasion of Poland many special Gypsy camps were evacuated to various Polish ghettos: in Litzmannstadt, Warsaw-Marymont, Kielce, Rabka, Zary, Siedlce,

---

* Professor Ritter was "denazified" in 1950.

Radom, Lublin, Hohensalza, Biala Podlaska, Wengrow. Many "biologically inferior" Gypsies were sent to the *Arbeitslager,* slave labor camps. Auschwitz, Birkenau and Mauthausen had specially enclosed *Zigeunerlager* where the Gypsies were allowed to live with their families and, being "interned but not arrested," were allowed to keep their personal possessions.

Minister of Propaganda Dr. Joseph Goebbels issued a *Direktive* about the treatment of *Untermenschen,* calling for *Vernichtung durch Arbeit*—extermination through labor. A later *Direktive* stated laconically, *"Soweit sie nicht mehr für kriegswichtige Arbeit zu gebrauchen waren"*—To the extent that they are no longer usable for essential war work. Late in 1941 Himmler took over from the Gestapo the running of the concentration camps. After the sterilization of *Fortplanzung-unwürdige Frauen* (women unworthy of human reproduction) began the *Vernichtung lebensunwürdigen Lebens*—destruction of life-unworthy lives.

There were three major waves of mass arrests of Gypsies in 1939, 1941, and 1943. First the Gypsies of Germany and Austria were "taken care of," then those from Poland, Czechoslovakia, Yugoslavia, the invaded territories of the Soviet Union, Holland, Belgium, Norway, and France, and last those from Hungary, Rumania, and Bulgaria. It is estimated that between 500,000 and 600,000 Gypsies perished.

In January, 1945, when the concentration camps in the east were evacuated by the Germans before the advancing Russians, many of the Gypsies who had survived until then and managed to escape were hunted down and shot by the SS and the Volkssturm, the German home defense army.

Whereas many aspects of the Jewish persecution and genocide are well known, the persecution and the extermination of the Gypsies has remained mostly undocumented. To a large extent this is due to the Gypsies' own lack of a sense of history. Even though over half a million of them were massacred, they are content to remain forgotten and unnoticed.

CHAPTER TWO

On the first day of the German invasion, when I had sighted the slow waves of Stukas as they tipped their wings and plunged to earth like black falcons, I was choked with the terrifying immediacy of war. I had been aware of an irretrievable loss, like death itself, leaving only a memory of innocence. Like everyone else, I submitted helplessly. Then I decided to act, to turn from the Rom. Having seen the luminous shore, I chose not to cross over to it. Military service would be my penance for having known too much happiness. I decided to cross the demarcation line which the Germans had established separating the occupied from "Free" France, and from there to cross into Spain. With luck on my side, I hoped to reach England to enlist. For the Rom the days of ceaseless travel were over.

With great circumspection I made my way to Paris, where I intended to contact a reliable friend of my parents who was usually well informed and realistic—the very progressive Mother Superior of an order of Catholic nuns.

The convent was in a dignified former mansion, on a wide tree-lined boulevard flanked on one side by the infamous prison of La Santé—a sinister presence in view of my subversive intentions. The hushed peace of the seemingly deserted convent evoked for me an era already vanished, somehow one of ghostly dated elegance. I wrote down my name in the guestbook, mentioned my parents' name as a reference and stated my request to see Mère Prieure. The silent, noncommittal nun left the reception area. When she came back she informed me in subdued, genteel, almost condescending tones that Mère Prieure was absent and that she would be absent for a prolonged period. I wondered why she had not told me this right away, but, in what I was sure must have been a contravention to the normal rules of the convent, I was offered hospitality for the night. This symbol of the closed world of women spelled out a safe and welcome haven.

The following day I haunted the area of *la Zone* around the Porte de Clignancourt and the Porte de St.-Ouen, where lived the Kalderash tribe whom I had visited only a few months earlier. In the hope of picking up gossip about illegal border traffic between France and Spain, I went to the *quartier* of the Plaine de St.-Denis where there were many Spanish refugees from the tragedy of the Civil War. At night I came back to the convent, but since I was not told I had to leave, I stayed another day and another and another. Every day I returned to the Zone and to the Plaine de St.-Denis. I hung around at the local Spanish barbershop, where my association with the Gypsies, known from an earlier date, stilled the Spaniards' initial distrust of me. The Gypsies were an integral part, if not a symbol of, the "twilight zone." I was able to listen in on the fairly unguarded conversations in Spanish, unguarded because they were held among a restricted group of trusted friends or acquaintances of long date who also happened to be customers. These Spanish refugees represented a wide spectrum of political shades but all adhered to the Loyalist cause. In this grim working-class district, sight, sound, and smell were strictly from Spain. There were *bodegas* and *carnicerías* and *dulces,* and the fashions of Spain were in nostalgic evidence everywhere. The neighborhood exuded a peculiar tang and a raucous quality evocative more of the Mediterranean than this gray decaying French *faubourg*. Severe-looking, gnarled women, perennially dressed in black, sat on their doorsteps. The men often wore short black leather jackets and corduroy trousers. Instead of the traditional *Buenos días* they greeted one another with the *Salud* of the Revolution. Hard faced and bristling with hostility, they were surly and quick tempered and there was a dark fire in their eyes. The majority were divested of all means of subsistence. They seemed to be exiled from the rest of humanity.

Through the warm windless air floated the sound of slightly frenetic *paso dobles* with that peculiarly glassy quality of a gramophone. It was my familiarity with the language, but also my parents' earlier social contacts with people involved in the Spanish Republican and Basque causes, that made it possible for me to penetrate the Spanish circles. There I learned from the survivors and absorbed some of the lessons of the tragic heroism of Spain, the betrayed hopes, the piteous martyrdom, the nameless terror. They summarized for me much of what I already knew and much that I did not know. The memories were still tragically fresh but already in the process of becoming the mythology of the Spanish Civil War. There was a stale lingering echo of proletarian meeting halls and there was vitriolic anticlericalism which during the war had been acted out in the sporadic profanation, looting, and wrecking of church property and ugly mass murders, sometimes as unwilled accidents of anarchy. At the back of the barbershop in the Plaine de St.-Denis district was a framed photograph, already a faded sepia color, of bearded militiamen with F.A.I. insignias. They wore their blankets rolled up, bandoleer fashion, across their shoulders. At José's I first saw the photograph of Dolores Ibarruri, the legendary La Pasionaria. Occasionally the men spoke with bitterness of the murderous internecine warfare. They also spoke about the Miranda de Ebro concentration camp and of police headquarters at the Puerta del Sol in Madrid and the torture of prisoners there. They spoke of those executed by the victor and of those who died in captivity and were officially labeled suicides. Under Nazi occupation they knew themselves to be marked men and made it a habit to sleep away from home. They spoke of the *contrabandistas,* the professional smugglers in the Pyrenees who helped maintain contact with Spain, for what it was worth, because for these men there was no choice on either side.

They were prone to wear party initials, pins, relics of times gone by, and I seemed to notice almost as many factions as there were ex-militiamen. At first I paid little attention to these esoteric distinctions. I could not help be aware of the Communists, Socialists, Trotskyites and Anarchists. I had heard about the Partido Obrero de Unificación Marxista and the Unión de los Hermanos Proletarios, but I was at a loss at first with U.G.T., C.N.T., J.C.I., J.S.U., F.A.I., P.S.U.C., etc. They knew themselves to be cornered animals with nowhere to go, except perhaps underground, for they were not the kind to give in. Watching, listening, I wondered at their sense of justice warped by despair and humiliation yet still obsessed with equivocal legalism.

Suddenly I discovered the beginning of a great loneliness. Many times I was given to understand that those I met and got to know were the few who, so far, had been lucky enough to avoid death or detention. I noticed a disproportionate number of women without men. Families were scattered. Many children had been temporarily placed with local families, some never to be reunited with their parents. The adults had hoped to find havens in France, England, America, or Russia but everywhere they had been embarrassingly unwelcome, as if people feared contagion from their despair, hunger, and grief.

Much of what I heard among the Spanish refugees was to me still the stuff of legends, fascinating but not completely relevant to everyday problems at hand, exceptions rather than the rule, though I deeply envied their seemingly absurd courage to continue the struggle despite insurmountable odds. Whenever the subject of the *contrabandistas* arose, or often when I tried to steer the conversation in that direction, I found specifics to be most elusive. Everyone felt the need to protect his sources. Aside from being keen to obtain a reliable contact with the *contrabandistas,* my secondary concern was to obtain fake French identification papers, without which traveling in the general direction of the Pyrenees would be difficult. I also needed indispensable demobilization certificates or else "proof" of my release from a prisoner-of-war camp. Without either of these I risked arrest.

On several occasions I was in contact with people who bragged about knowing someone who in turn knew someone else who made or could procure false documents or, better yet, who claimed to *maquiller,* to alter or adapt genuine but stolen identification papers. The conditions were cash on the spot and the amount was substantial, though the sums mentioned varied disturbingly. But above all else, no questions were to be asked. All dealings were handled through go-betweens whose reliability seemed more than doubtful. I was aware that even if the documents were delivered to me—and what guarantee of this did I have, after all?—I could not evaluate the expertise of the falsification or how well they would pass the crucial test of authenticity when my life would come to depend on them. I knew my vulnerability and helplessness in this descent to the netherworld of criminality. By definition this was a world of deception and violence. I dreaded being at the mercy of petty amateur criminals and coffeehouse strategists posing strength or cunning. It proved more difficult than I had anticipated to track down contacts, and their stories and specific promises were forever receding or shifting. I was bothered by their obsessive lack of forth-rightness and their quickness to resent supposed slights to their "honor," or for that matter their overly confidential airs, their "to be quite frank with you" or "tell you the whole truth," natural introductions to transparent lies. I was frustrated and in despair, yet totally unable to swallow the bait.

I was tempted to turn for help to the Gypsies, but having made my break with Pulika and the Lowara, I felt moral compunctions about turning to the Rom for assistance. I knew they were not experts on forgery or counterfeit but rather for what I sensed must be their value as potential psychological "equalizers." Acting as part of the group, or posing at it, I felt might substantially reduce the risks of being cheated—because of the reputed Gypsy revenge. I gained a renewed insight into the many-faceted defense mechanism of the Rom, which to them had become a second nature. I saw in a new light their need to project a specific image, often fiercer than the reality. I saw the strange usefulness of an occasional totally contradictory image, adding to the confusion of outsiders. They were experienced enough to know not to do this only in times of pressure and immediate need, but at all times and automatically, to prevent rather than to cure.

From day to day I postponed making a decision about the

fake papers or to entrust to anyone else, to any of the "experts," the regulation-size photographs of myself.

Before curfew I discreetly slipped back to the convent. One evening I returned to my monastic hideaway to find a stranger waiting for me. A melancholy half-smile was the only apology he offered for his intrusion or as explanation for his presence in my cell-like room. I do not remember if it was the implied feeling of security in the hushed convent atmosphere or his gentle reticent appearance which put me at ease, but I did not sense a threat. I wondered why the nun who opened the door to the outside world had let him pass and why she had not cared to inform me about him. As always she had been silent and noncommittal.

The curtains were open and the light had not been turned on. In the half-light the man looked of average stature, early middle-aged, vaguely distinguished, scholarly perhaps. It struck me that his hands were well cared for. When he spoke he revealed himself as more self-assured than his unassuming mien had led me to expect. His voice was slightly nasal and betrayed a trace of an accent, though it could have been regional French, possibly from the Auvergne. I never found out where he hailed from. He wore a conservative slightly threadbare double-breasted suit. His right eye focused ever so little outward and appeared larger than his left. His attitude allayed my distrust. His intent was clear and direct. Though I have forgotten his exact choice of words, he proposed that I become a liaison operative between the Gypsies and "them," who I unquestioningly assumed were the British. There was no room for either yes or no. He never asked. In a way I was flattered by the attention but equally puzzled that anyone should be aware of my relationship to the Rom. Also, whoever he was, he had been well informed to know where to contact me. The thought of unknowingly having been under surveillance was disturbing. Yet again this was the inescapable reality.

The man never told me his name and I did not find it out until much later. What he proposed was nothing less than the active participation of the Gypsies in anti-German activities. His approach and development of these ideas were well thought out and showed great capacity for anticipation. Despite this, I felt that some of his concepts smacked more of poetry than subversive intelligence or underground warfare. He was half visionary, half introvert. Modestly elusive, he was boldly frank when he was obliged to deal with brutal facts. What he had to say stirred me sufficiently to accept his proposition, even though I felt grossly inadequate for the task and was fully aware that it carried no reward and possibly a great deal of penalty. Yet I accepted it as a compliment both to the Rom and to me.

He initiated me into the ideology of dissent and I willingly accepted apprenticeship. At first he expounded simplified formulations in a need to condense and to summarize. What to me, a neophyte, seemed to glare as the weaker parts in the structure were due to an understandable cultural gap between Gaje and Rom. He was aware of this and willingly submitted to my criticism, while at the same time testing my resourcefulness and my willingness. He broke off abruptly and with his curious melancholy half-smile said "they" had decided to use as our recognition phrase *"Mortem servituti antepone"*—death before slavery. He quietly left my room, letting me close the door behind him.

I knew we would meet again, but no time or date had been set. It occurred to me that perhaps this was an oversight. Or was it?

In the streets of Paris the curfew was still in force and while I wondered why he had left so suddenly I found myself equally concerned about his safety after hours in the German controlled city. Perhaps he was simply absentminded, but then again how could he be in his profession? Stirred as I was, I was at the mercy of my youthful exuberance and undisciplined imagination. I left the curtains open. Though it was pitch dark I did not turn on the night light for fear of reversing the illusion.

I slept fitfully and once, waking from a half-slumber, I wondered if my evening visitor had not simply been a hallucination. I spent the following day and evening waiting. I did not want to leave in case he tried to contact me again. There was no one I could talk to or confide in, with whom I could share my excitement. Though the visitor had not actually imposed secrecy, I felt it by implication. Once I tried to engage in conversation with the silent doorwarder-nun. She condescendingly ignored me and rushed on in a rustling of her voluminous black habit.

To pass the day and still my anxieties, I washed my socks, underwear, and only shirt. I washed my handkerchief and, as substitute for ironing, flattened it out wet against the smooth surface of the mirror. Furtively I polished my shoes with the reverse side of the cotton bedspread. I pressed my trousers after the fashion of the thrifty western European travelers by putting them neatly folded under my mattress overnight. Unconsciously I must have tried to emulate my new mentor's urbane anonymity in contrast to the rugged, disheveled, baggy, nonchalant appearance of my earlier Gypsy associates.

On the third day of waiting I went for a walk. During my self-imposed seclusion I thought not so much about the need for open resistance to the Germans, but rather about the immediate feasibility and effectiveness of it. Now the sight of German soldiers, guidebook in hand, sightseeing through the streets of Paris, made me ambiguously sad for them and chafing for action to oppose them ruthlessly.

I was looking out into the darkening street from behind the daytime lace curtain so as not to be noticed from the outside when he came in, coughing softly to announce his arrival. He waited for me to invite him to sit down, a little formality before resuming the conversation interrupted without warning several days before. No explanation was given. He simply returned to the main train of thought about what could, and urgently should, be done to confound the enemy; and to confound the enemy, he implied with quiet scholarly conviction, justified almost any degree of violence and the use of any weapon. Unemotionally (it seemed almost patiently) he emphasized that the weapons at our disposal were not a matter of our own choosing. He sounded like a doctor advising a patient about unavoidable major surgery. Then again with self-effacing modesty he would speak of "them," of what "they" suggested, wanted, hoped, and expected. During this he reverted to sober analytical methodology. For a moment I would have a brief blurred glimpse of an ambitious overall structure. On other occasions he would lose my focused attention. My thoughts wandered off as the seeming grandness of the schemes made them appear unattainable. Then, with expressions of irony and affection, he would patiently make allowances and narrow down the focus of his exposition. He would leave the wider implications in order to involve me, prying out my reservations, my doubts, the why of my indifference. He would give specific hints of what could be done and how.

I stayed on at my convent retreat. No questions were asked about the duration of my stay; for that matter, no questions of any kind were ever asked. The only person with whom I came into contact was the nun in charge of the door. The faint whispering of female voices, the rustling of bulky robes, and subdued footsteps hurrying down the long corridors were as close as I ever came to seeing or meeting any of my neighbors, which in view of my irregular status as a guest suited me to perfection.

Our daily indoctrination-study sessions became a pleasant routine. Pure theory was only rarely disrupted by furtive visions of mangled flesh and blood. He was a relentless taskmaster, but at times I wished it could simply go on this way forever. I noticed he never indulged in small talk or ever allowed our relationship to become personal or familiar in any way. It was he who led me through my formative experience in this wartime twilight zone. It was he who inspired me to become an agent, yet I knew nothing about him. To me he was like the operating surgeon on whom one's life depends, who seen through the haze of anesthesia remains only a masked outline of a figure, yet uncannily familiar and affecting. I fully trusted him and refrained from expressing or feeling any doubt or asking pertinent questions.

Because of his systematic and patient elaborations, I would sometimes imagine that he might be a mathematician, but then again because of his subtlety it occurred to me that he might be a linguist. At other times his relentless clearly formulated inquiry into the social organization and psychology of the Rom made me opt for social anthropology as his discipline, yet he expressed himself in a direct way free of specialist's jargon. He was detached yet concerned, remote yet searching, intellectually restless, yet in chilling contrast to his meek appearance he was pragmatic to the point of ruthlessness. His unfaltering discernment and accuracy of observation awed me and with arrogant modesty I allowed myself to be flattered by the communion of thought I felt existed between us.

With anthropological sophistication he did not equate the Gypsies' illiteracy with lack of intelligence; he referred to them as preliterate. He seemed to easily grasp the Gypsies' sense of constant flux and change. In trying to enroll them in the wider movement of resistance to the Germans he was well aware both of the advantages their way of life offered and equally of their built-in limitations. He intimated that for most people the habits of a lifetime could not be changed in a short period. He never underestimated the tactical struggle for everyday survival. His perception of the world of the Gypsies was free of my own unduly prismatic distortion of it. He merely smiled to express doubt or disagreement. He never argued or condemned.

I was aware that before approaching me my tutor must have also subjected me to scrutiny. I suspected that he must have known of my personal sense of confusion and my guilt at leaving the Rom at this particular time, as if I were fleeing my share of their pain when their destiny was most precarious, and of my equally guilty wish to be reunited with the group again. I was particularly grateful to him not to probe or dwell on this but instead to offer me the opportunity to exorcise it. He led me to feel that in the present tragedy of German conquest and hegemony, engulfing all and threatening to obliterate the slow accumulation of centuries of Western humanism, there was an opportunity for me to lose, or prove, myself in action. It rang in my ears with a decisive sense of fatality, like the fall one cannot prevent. No more would I feel myself like the dog with the broken back I once saw on a dusty country road after a fight, turning in dizzying circles to outrun its pain.

In need of refreshment, I tried to draw my mentor into postwar speculation. Quietly, without reproof, he spoke instead of the imperatives of the moment, that present without which no tomorrow was possible and which under the imposed conditions demanded our indifference to all values we had learned to cherish. For an instant his inspired look waned, as if suddenly dried up, and his "presence" seemed to shrink. He said that under abnormal circumstances an abnormal reaction, that is one of total violence, was normal and therefore imperative. We should renounce life out of our love for life, in order to prevent it from becoming a blasphemy. He then added, as an unguarded afterthought, "if we survive . . ." The sentence remained unfinished, completed by his apologetic half-smile. Could it be that he too had to resist the temptation of hope and the distraction of doubts?

Only by accepting our role unconditionally could we function efficiently. "We must free ourselves from life, from all the possibilities of life, of all the temptations worth living for. We must consider it as an act of God and know there is no need to think." What he demanded from me was in a sense the very renunciation of faith in the rationality of man as well as total mystical dedication to a ruthless secretive commitment!

Faraway muffled chanting of the monastery choir brought me back with a vengeance to a different reality with its alluring melancholy peace and deceiving resignation. This intrusion was like a hallucination of the Black Mass. My mentor seemed not to hear—or at least not to pay attention—to this reminder of a more commonly accepted morality. With self-willed myopia, he doggedly returned to what could be done and how to do it. He combined a clinical detachment with the logic of passion.

He urged me to direct all my energies, passions, and thoughts into one obsessive goal: to create conditions of insecurity, chaos, and unrest for the Germans by all and any means, choosing or improvising whatever methods were most suitable to the particular opportunity or challenge presenting itself. He showed me a spectrum of possibilities while allowing for unanticipated situations where on-the-spot decisions would be required. There was, after all, no substitute for experience; there were things one learned that could not be taught. At first I should content myself to help catalyze diffuse sources of dissent, taking advantage of general discontent and progressive disenchantment, establish contacts, weld together fragmentary fringe groups, stir the collective imagination of the Rom, fan sparks into sustained fire, into eventual concerted action, keep smoldering the sense of violence, and at least for the time being, avoid any kind of leadership.

After allowing me another few days, he informed me one evening, in seemingly casual fashion, that I must return to the Gypsies the following day. As he was about to leave he handed me a set of French identity papers, demobilization documents, proof of present employment, and various recommendations made out in the name of one Henri Vandries, born in the Pas-de-Calais, which would partially "explain" my Flemish accent. There was a substantial sum of money in various denominations. He told me I should come back to Paris as soon as I felt I possessed the "necessary elements" to talk further about "our plans"—whenever I had established sufficient contacts to make action possible. I should simply come to the convent and wait there to be contacted by him. With what I sensed as a tinge of reluctance he added that if necessary he would see to it that I was contacted "wherever" I happened to be. I could not guess at what he really meant and he did not elaborate.

CHAPTER THREE

I returned to the Gypsies. I reached the temporary encampment at dusk. A small cluster of wagons was partly hidden from the road by a row of stubby, disheveled knotty willows. With elation I recognized the familiar outlines of horses between the trees. Instead of the wildly blazing campfires that had been common before the beginning of the hostilities, there now were only some smoldering embers with buckets of water or heaps of dirt at the ready to extinguish them in case of airplane alert.

The night was chill after a hot day. There was a smell of animal muskiness, of leather, sweat, and smoke, of wet straw and horsedung. I found a renewed taste in life in the fraternity of the bivouac, with the ever-changing intensity of the sky overhead. To celebrate my return I let myself be lulled in a state of contemplative serenity. We sat by the small heap of dying embers and talked late into the night. Gradually I caught up on current news and gossip about the Rom traveling everywhere about the countryside. Pulika and Rupa were well and I resolved that as soon as enough time had passed to satisfy the conventions of Romani hospitality I would leave my present hosts and join my adopted parents. We talked about how the German occupation affected the Rom. They said that except for some material restrictions life for them was much as before. The Gypsies were left to roam the countryside at will and no new restrictions had been imposed on them—as yet. In the prevailing chaos and scramble they appeared to have been forgotten. Judging from the meal I shared with them, my hosts did not seem to suffer much from the rather drastic food rationing that plagued city people.

The night sky was clear and full of stars and for the first time in many weeks I was able to surrender totally to the mercy of serene sleep. Suddenly the dry barking of antiaircraft batteries fairly close by jolted me awake and reminded me inexorably of the presence of war. Searchlight beams probed the darkness, searching, triangulating, sweeping.

In the morning, life among the Gypsies once again exerted for me its potent attraction, numbing me with contentment. Night thoughts faded away; doubts lost their impact and urgency. Leisurely the Gypsies broke camp and the wagons jolted along the rutted dirt road. We traveled through dark moist forest filled with the smell of moss, leaves, and decaying fruit. Life among the Gypsies reflected freedom, wildness, endless space, and the haunting temptation of uncomplicated happiness. However, I could not fully push back the feeling that reassurance was strictly deceitful. I knew I was only trying to forget something else; and yet my main concern was not avoiding pain or, for that matter, gaining pleasure, but rather my growing awareness of needing something to live for. By formulating and sharing with me his vision, my nameless taskmaster offered to shoulder part of the responsibility for the empirical validation of his concept of resistance, leaving me no longer completely without moorings and with a short-range goal. Not only did he cut off my escape into the past but he helped me increasingly to expunge my already wavering allegiance to the Gypsies, without thereby in any way lessening my budding nostalgia for what I could no longer be part of. I vainly tried to rekindle what already had become memories.

We traveled for several days, occasionally meeting other small Gypsy bands at overnight camping sites. As I totally immersed myself in Gypsy life, I noticed myriad minor changes in pattern of their lives, like the absence after dark of fires which would have unduly attracted the attention of the Germans and might have been interpreted by them as flare signals for incoming British bombers. We were bothered by mosquitoes now more than in the past; it occurred to me that before the war, when fires were permissible after dark, the smoke kept them away. The Rom also had broken up their large units into smaller bands to lessen the danger of detection and contact with the occupation forces. I could not help notice that the young men stayed out of sight, as did most young women and attractive girls for that matter. Most visible at all times were the old crones, who often displayed defiant tooth-less grins. They were surrounded by the unconsciously pro-vocative display of well-fed naked brown babies, which did not make the absence of youth any more believable. In the rare unavoidable contacts with the Germans, the old ones played the inarticulate, baffled, baited animal, gaining in security what they seemed to lose in dignity. With an uncanny sense of their collective destiny, even the otherwise intractable Tshurara tribe seemed, for a time, to have mended their rambunctious ways, curbing their perpetual itch for plunder. Only in the intimacy of camp was the normal sumptuous dis-play of colors to be savored in an orgy of cobalts, indigos, scarlets, sulphurs, rubies, ultramarines, ochres, and sepias, highlighted by a furtive show of gold. This explosion of color was itself set against the background of rich foliage. The men wore mostly dark brown or gray corduroy and wide-brimmed black hats, with strong color in the kerchief knotted at their throats. In the seclusion and privacy of their quarters the Gypsies still reflected an enviable, seemingly carefree ex-uberance.

One day we caught up with Pulika and his band. Suddenly I was home again and glad to be back.

The night was windless and the air heavy with the strong intoxicating fragrance of honeysuckle mixed with the smoke of a smoldering woodfire. It was deeply reassuring to see Pulika and I realized again the extent to which, during the years I had spent with the Rom, he had become for me the symbol of manliness, of love, and hunger for life. The Gypsy men around him were truly men and their women were equally and fully women.

Not long before, I had left Pulika's people with the firm intention of volunteering for military duty under British com-

mand. I mistakenly thought then that I was emotionally detached from the Rom. My return to the Rom stirred me more
than I had anticipated, causing me to wonder why I had
wanted to leave them in the first place. I left the Rom sincerely
believing my departure was final and irreversible, when an
unexpected combination of circumstances and timing deflected my course, superseding my original plans. I returned to
the Gypsies with a specific, though nascent, mission as a
liaison operative.

I hoped this might help redeem earlier absences from my
Gaje background and my seeming lack of concern and responsibility in the face of what, even to me, was a rather
inappropriate vocational pursuit, that of simply "being a
Gypsy." After six years of growing up among the Rom (with
extended visits to my parents), Pulika had offered me total
integration into his tribe through marriage and I had realized
my reluctance toward total commitment. I may have been
swayed partly by my concern about disappointing my parents,
who had allowed me an extraordinary amount of personal
freedom at a very early age and who had let me mature at my
own pace. There may have been some purely pragmatic considerations as well—second thoughts about a future as an
itinerant horse dealer. I needed to participate in cultural life
beyond that of the nomadic horde while I envied the ethno-
centrism I could not wholeheartedly share.

Except for my father's implicit wish that I become an artist,
I had no aspiration toward any particular profession. By force
of circumstances my secondary education had been badly
neglected, which did not simplify matters. At best, following
my father's example, I was inclined toward art. On the one
hand the desperate and worsening world situation, and on the
other the inordinate spell of the Gypsies, had done little to
help me clarify my position or encourage me to act positively.
The threat of military conscription had further hampered me
in facing reality and, between fits of painting and sculpting
when at my parents' home, I had simply extemporated.

Time and circumstances had caught up with me. After restlessly shifting back and forth I had come back to the Rom in

an unexpected prolongation of my youth. Because of the war, a future of my own seemed far removed and unrelated. The task I had accepted—attempting to actively involve the Gypsies in the war effort—would not be easy. Therefore, instead of dissociating myself from the Rom I had to reintegrate with them.

Facing Pulika, I had misgivings about my task, an uneasy feeling of betrayal toward him and his people: one of profanation, of ulterior motive, and wanting to use them for the Gaje's purposes. Squatting on their heels around the faintly glowing embers, Pulika and the other Rom were smoking, drinking, and talking. The horses stood in clusters nearby and everything was peaceful. The war and the German conquerors seemed to be far away, but despite lapses into forgetfulness they could not be forgotten.

Eventually Pulika got up to "look at the horses" (the Lowara euphemism for answering the call of nature) and wished the other men good night as he ambled away. I followed him and Kore into the clear summer night. I was anxious to be alone with him while at the same time I felt more and more confused—fearing the very confrontation I had so desperately longed for. How could I tell him the reason for my return to the Rom? The world of the Rom and that of the Gaje truly could never meet.

Walking slowly to the meadow a few paces behind him, I was deeply aware of his presence. Like a dream within a dream, my recent initiation flashed before me in violent contrast. Pulika imperceptibly slowed his pace, letting Kore go ahead in the direction of the stationary troop of horses. Concealing the flare of the match in the palm of his hand, Pulika lit a hand-rolled cigarette. The semidarkness and his feigned indifference brought an unanticipated climax. He listened without surprise and I thought I noticed a smile under the cover of his fierce mustache as I talked volubly and at random. I calmed down considerably as I unburdened myself. Some of the things I tried to tell him no longer made any sense even to me. They sounded like fantasies and I had difficulty interpreting them to him. Nevertheless, I preserved a narrow zone of silence—reticence, if not of intended secrecy. The unreal world of the Gaje was far away indeed and irrelevant, yet I felt the necessity to minimize, in fact to misrepresent, to Pulika my feelings. I felt foolish and apologetic but I also knew the spreading war had as much relevance for the Rom as for the rest of humanity.

Pulika held the butt of his cigarette between thumb and index finger, concealing the glowing end in the cupped palm of his hand. I had grown silent and for a while we stood there in the half dark meadows, Pulika's legs akimbo. When he spoke his voice was unusually low but steady; he spoke as he did when dealing with frightened or recalcitrant horses. In his monologue—in which he endearingly referred to me in the third person—he said, "Avidity for fortune-telling comes from an inability to cope with your anxieties, and its indulgence creates a self-perpetuating greed for more 'prophecy.' " Though I listened intently I failed to see what fortune-telling could possibly have to do with my being contacted by British Intelligence or their interest in involving the Gypsies in anti-German activities.

"Fortune-telling is more harmful than compulsive gambling," he went on, "because in gambling all you stand to lose is money. In fortune-telling there is no gain at all, but you lose insight into yourself in a vain search for magic solutions to problems, especially since the problems are caused by an unwillingness to face life as it is." I realized that he was questioning my motivation rather than reflecting on the proposal. "I know your distress," Pulika said. "I know you are overwhelmed by the feeling of entrapment, that order, reason, and justice are no more. Despite everything, you, like so many others, can not bring yourself to admit to human wickedness."

Seemingly out of context, as was his way, Pulika continued. "Never eat food as hot as it is cooked. Remember, some years ago, when you and Kore were shot at by the old farmer and you were hit by salt pellets? Remember how angry you were at the 'injustice' done to you, or as you said then, to *us*, the Rom, even though you and the other boys were raiding the farmer's apple orchard?"

I did remember. My anger had been in sharp contrast to Kore's fatalism. Kore slept and recovered rapidly while I brooded. When I had informed Pulika of my intention to go back to the village to put fire to their haystacks, he listened gravely, without interrupting me. The futility of my urge for "justice" and my way to achieve it became apparent. Instead of allowing me to carry out what I meant to do, Rupa and Keja had gone back to the village, at Pulika's suggestion, alone and by night. They had put a "Gypsy curse" on the offender and his property. The women fully realized that the effectiveness of their action was based solely on the Gaje's underlying fear of Gypsy curses and spells. The Rom always said it was better to frighten a man than to injure him. Their primary objective was survival.

Fantastically shaped black clouds chased each other against a pewter-gray yet inexplicably luminous night sky. The black clouds hurrying by over the high treetops were haloed by backlighting, disquieting, otherworldly, conjuring the unforgotten image of a stormy sea seen in a hallucination.

For a while Pulika and I smoked in silence with a complete sense of detachment from the war, oblivious to the necessity for haste and urgency. When Pulika resumed his monologue his voice seemed warmer and more intimate than before.

"In these times a man should resist being seduced by death. He should not face the morning sun as if it were already night! Heroism is to stay alive in the face of danger and dare to love.

"Man needs woman to lend compassion to his manhood, to protect him from the temptation of hurting others, to allow him the chance to ripen and to define himself, to become a *man*. The measure of a man is his willingness to accept responsibility. Your fulfillment shall be according to the extent of your hunger—for even from the mightiest river the stallion can drink only his fill. You should under no circumstances tolerate bitterness in place of happiness."

For a fugitive instant I felt myself swayed by the flood of Pulika's lyrical exaltation. I knew him as a man and as a father, I had observed him as a husband, I respected him as the responsible head of an extended family, but I had not suspected in him this particular lyrical fervor. As his resolution overcame mine, I allowed myself to dream of the felicity of married life. The distress inherent in this dream shocked me. I suddenly discovered a desperate, boundless longing for a life that made sense. Then I caught again the sound of Pulika's voice.

"To me," he said, "history is one unending flow of statistics of equally unending wars. For every positive experiment, entire populations have to perish.

"Putzina, do not accept their ideological passions. There are lies, as you know, more easily believed than truth, and courage about death often disguises cowardice about life. Leave to others the quest for eternal certainties. Learn to accept that there are questions that have no answers. Man should be able to live with his experiences and with himself. If a tree is straight what does it matter if to some it appears crooked?"

Without any apparent transition from his previous train of thought, Pulika then said, "You should go back and establish your contact more firmly. We need a link. Without outside help, resistance would be much more difficult."

Pulika fell silent again, but it was a while before the silence became noticeable. The restless neighing of the horses brought me out of my introspection. It was answered by the cry, at once doleful and tender, of an unseen bird in some nearby linden trees. In the gray dawn we walked toward the encampment in silence to sleep for a few hours before the new day started. As I lay on the large featherbed under the open sky I felt proud, strong, and very calm.

CHAPTER FOUR

The days that followed were uneventful. We traveled short distances each day, remaining within a limited radius and off the much-used arteries. Pulika and Yojo went to the local inns or visited the village blacksmiths and those local horsedealers who had not been displaced by the war or deported. The Gypsy women and children remained out of sight as much as was possible. The skills the Rom used before the war to "improve" the appearance of the horses in our possession were now used to deliberately downgrade or hide whatever qualities they had and thus minimize the danger of confiscation. Possibly this was also done so as not to awaken the envy and greed of local farmers, who might have been less lucky in this respect.

Fortune-telling and begging were discouraged. We sat by the light of the moon and the stars and, when the nights were chill, by the barely visible smoldering embers of campfires. During the summer of 1940 the weather was most pleasant and the nights on the whole clear and warm.

Never during my life among the Gypsies had I observed greater circumspection. As we moved about we found fresh *vurmi* (trailside messages) left by other traveling Gypsies. We also left well-disguised messages, but somehow we never met up with the others.

In the cities, food, clothing, and other necessities were severely rationed or more often simply unavailable. City people would trek to the countryside by bicycle—there was no gasoline for private cars—to buy directly from the farmers the produce they managed at risk to withhold from government requisitions. Because of the scarcity and the danger in illegal dealings, food prices became exorbitant. Unlike the peasants and the urban poor, who traditionally kept their savings in cached currency, the urban population put its money in bank savings accounts which became controlled or even completely frozen by the occupiers. As available cash ran out, the population reverted to bartering citified luxuries for plain country food. Soon the farmers found themselves glutted with superfluities and the gloss of novelty wore off. Signs were surreptitiously displayed advising potentially outraged customers that only silver and gold would be accepted.

Returning to the cities, many of the adventurous buyers were intercepted by the local constabulary and their illegal acquisitions of bread, butter, eggs, bacon, potatoes, or dried beans were summarily seized as contraband, conceivably for the gendarmes' personal benefit. Protest or resistance led only to further unpleasantness. People slowly learned to be more devious, and from necessity arose a new spirit of defiance.

Pulika and Yojo easily managed to provide their families with staple food. However, there was a dearth of industrially produced or centrally distributed products such as sugar, tea, coffee, salt, condiments, tobacco, shoes, and clothes. When available at all, these could be obtained only in exchange for special ration stamps which were issued anew every month. In order to obtain these—and without them not even bread or potatoes were to be had—everyone had to register. Afterward, even changing domicile was forbidden without permission of the German Kommandant. Every move was controlled and duly recorded. Every single person could be traced and, when the need arose, tracked down.

After some understandable initial hesitation, Pulika and the other Rom registered. I went along with Pulika and observed in amazement how he registered his dependents under the legitimate Dutch name of van der Meulen, producing documents to match. But used to the wondrous ways of the Rom, I abstained from comment. As long as I had lived with them I believe I had seen Pulika use his status as a stateless person exclusively to advantage, to obtain when necessary proper *ad hoc* identification papers and travel documents.

A few days later Pulika registered again, in a different locality and under a different name, this time presenting apparently valid Hungarian passports. I remember that these were under the name of Vadosh. Some members of the family were under the name Korpats. Yet when he decided to register once again under yet another name, I started to fear for his, and our own, security. However, this *ruse de guerre* went undetected and in the midst of severe rationing and penury the Rom of our *kumpania* lived in comparative affluence. They bartered their surplus sugar, soap, and textile allowances. In the process they established a new kind of relationship with the farmers, since the peasants had fairly plentiful products of the land (difficult to control) but relatively little of anything else.

These days the Rom dressed a little more conservatively than had been their custom. They claimed to be Armenians, Arabs true to the mufti of Jerusalem, or else they posed as South American businessmen and they managed a certain credibility in any new role as long as women or children remained out of sight, for they were the undeniable telltale that would identify the men for what they really were. They made it a point to single themselves out as not being Spanish, to avoid being taken for refugees of the Spanish Civil War.

One day we learned that a large horde of Gypsies, the *kumpania* of old Tshurka, had been rounded up by the Germans in the Netherlands. We had crossed his path many times and knew him and his people well. Unlike many other vanquished nations ruled by their own nationals collaborating with the Germans, Holland had refused to accommodate and in consequence had been taken over completely by the victors and was run rigidly by an all-German apparatus. The Dutch countryside consisted to a great extent of intensively cultivated flatlands and grazing meadows, devoid of forests and lending itself badly to ensconcement and evasive seclusion. Baba Tshurka, we were told, had produced perfectly legal

Nicaraguan passports. Since Nicaragua at that time was still a neutral country—and as such the Germans had an interest in courting it—the Rom had been promptly released. They were provided with German *laissez-passer* facilitating their free circulation. For a while they were freer than before, but then, along with the U.S.A., Nicaragua declared war upon Germany and the Baba Tshurkeshti, as they called themselves, were interned for the duration of the war as "enemy aliens." They were treated well and "protected" under the Geneva Agreement conventions. Most other Gypsies living in the Netherlands at that time, the majority of whom happened to be Sinti, were deported to the east—never to return.

During those first few months of the German occupation the attitude and relationship between the Gypsies and the farmers changed considerably. They were drawn together by the menacing presence of a common enemy. Until then the Rom had been aliens speaking an alien tongue. Now they traded together in rationed goods and farm produce and developed a common bond of interest. When the occasion arose, they warned one another of impending police raids. As the press was heavily censored and there was, besides, a dearth of regional news, they would exchange gossip and stories, information and rumors. At that time the Gypsies still moved about at will and they agreed to pass on messages and run occasional errands as personal favors. The Rom had lived all their lives in some form of emergency and therefore knew the tactics of survival. They adjusted easily to the drastically changed psychological climate. As before the war, they continued to build vast networks of "contacts" and to consolidate existing "friendships" in line with present and long range needs.

One evening at a roadside inn, the owner-barkeeper took Pulika aside and with conspiratorial airs asked him in roundabout fashion if the Rom would consider dealing with "some friends of his" to transport a cargo of illegal goods, and what their price for it would be. At first Pulika tried to banter with him about sharing equally what he assumed would be huge profits. As he put it in Romani, when telling us the story later, "to tell a lie is the best way to learn the truth." In no time the man was babbling out, much against his better judgment, that it was he himself who wanted to have the Rom transport a strictly nonprofit *human* cargo. Pulika said that if such were the case he would do it only "as a friend," which to be sure carried its fringe benefits and might even in time have proved a worthwhile investment. To seal the agreement they drank some good prewar brandy and no further questions were asked.

That night several Gaje came to our small camp under cover of darkness. Several of our young boys had been posted to keep the dogs from barking too wildly or attacking them. The men only stayed a short while and when they left one of them stayed behind. After a last drink of water, Yojo let him crawl into the large storage bin suspended underneath the wagon in which the Rom usually kept spare harnesses, chains, and tools. It had a hinged door and was secured with a padlock.

We left early the next morning and traveled in our habitual erratic pattern as if nothing were unusual. I forgot about the entire incident until the following night when I saw Yojo let the stranger out from his confined hideout and take him for a walk. He brought him food and water and somewhat later locked him in again. I wondered if he had been fed at all during the day. After a few days I noticed he was no longer taken out to stretch his legs, to relieve himself, or to be fed and I realized that unnoticed by me he must already have been delivered to his destination somewhere along the road.

On several other occasions Pulika or other members of our *kumpania* provided clandestine transportation for fugitives. The Rom had a peculiarly Romany way of doing things (seemingly erratic and unorganized) so that one was never fully aware of specific subversive acts or involvements. Since they always lived on the borderline of illegality anyway, they accepted with greater ease the present circumstances of added stress and risk.

Late one night several wagons arrived and set up their

overnight camp near a farmhouse beside a mountain stream. The night was clear and we could easily make out the sprawling tobacco-drying sheds with their long peaked roofs and open latticework sides. I understood from Pulika that on the following day we were to make a pickup in the vicinity. He did not specify anything further. It was already late and, since it was ill advised to light fires after dark, we went to sleep without our evening meal. The next morning several of us were already up at dawn, grilling freshly caught trout over a small fire of pine needles. From a short distance we saw several black cars full of determined-looking men in dark clothes drive by uphill at breakneck speed. We heard the shriek of brakes and what sounded to us like a rifle report, and then not too far away a female wail of pain. We were at the edge of the forest and below us we could see fertile bottom lands. Instinctively the Rom gathered the bedding and stored it hurriedly inside the wagons. They fetched the grazing horses to harness them and make the wagons ready for flight.

I remember suddenly noticing in an irrelevant closeup a purple and silver thistle growing next to our smoldering fire. This peaceful vision and the equally pastoral smell of burning pine needles were both in sharp contrast to the tragic events happening nearby. Soon afterward the sinister-looking black cars drove by again at leisure. As they passed our encampment the lead car slowed as if to stop. The determined-looking men in their dark suits and raincoats looked less tense, some even appeared almost relaxed. The man sitting next to the driver leaned out of the window to better look at us. They spoke roughly but we could not make out what they said. In any case we guessed it was not intended to be friendly or reassuring. They laughed uproariously, but their laughter betrayed no joy or pleasure. After a hesitation the car abruptly speeded up again and they disappeared, leaving behind clouds of dust.

Even in our understandable consternation, we had briefly spied the prisoners framed between the men—who else could they have been but the Gestapo? The prisoners looked gray and shrunken by fear. Their eyes were filmed with shock and despair, comatose, yet they held a look of helpless pleading. Keja claimed afterward she had seen small children among them. As on many similar occasions, I had been shocked by the incredible discrepancy between the hunters and the hunted, between the butchers and their victims. Unreasoningly, we hastily broke camp. To the Rom, proximity and association with disaster or violence made for *marhime,* taboo.

As we drove by, none of the Rom looked in the direction of the farmhouse. But I did. The doors and windows had been left open, emphasizing its desertion. Since the inhabitants were gone, perhaps forever, my concern seemed irrelevant yet strangely affecting. For a little while longer the faint wisp of gray smoke would rise from the chimney. The geraniums were in full bloom. Passing through the hamlet below, where everybody had already been alerted about the raid, we gleaned scattered bits of information. The people arrested during the raid had been part of a vast illegal organization rumored to have been helping men escape from German-occupied territory in order to join the Allied fighting forces in England. We also learned what seemed to be common knowledge, that the tobacco farmer had been betrayed by a "friend turned enemy." In retaliation the Germans had arrested not only the men they found in hiding, but also the farmer's entire family and any other people found under his roof at the time of the raid, regardless of the reasons for their presence.

A few days later some local gendarmes were routinely checking the Gypsies' travel documents. One of them detached himself from their group and slowly walked over to Pulika's wagon. With his boot he ostentatiously kicked the door of the storage bin suspended beneath the wagon. No police officer had ever shown any interest in the contraption. The way in which he did this seemed too nonchalant not to be premeditated. In an even subdued tone he asked what was inside. It was obvious that he was acting on inside information. Keja, who was standing nearby, shrugged her shoulders, seemingly unbothered, and said that we had lost the keys to it long ago. Kore added that it was of no use to us in its present state, locked up, and inquired if by chance there was a locksmith in the nearby village. As an afterthought he added that for that matter a hardware store would do, for a hacksaw. The constable lost interest. He went away without further botherment. For all I know, the officer, far from being a villain as we suspected, may even have been attempting to warn us. Under the cover of dusk Kore let out the stranger who had been hiding there. He walked him in the direction of the grazing land where the horses were and let him smoke. When food was ready Yojo brought him some of it away from the camp and the other Rom. I suspect that later that night he was locked in again and taken along to be surrendered wherever it had been agreed for him to be delivered.

Slowly but inexorably the Rom were becoming involved in a variety of illegal activities mainly connected with smuggling of people or of rationed goods; sooner or later they would become involved this way in transporting explosives and small arms. By this time, many men were living in hiding, either for their personal safety or because of their involvement with Resistance activities, and thus were disqualified from drawing ration cards, which in turn made it impossible to get food at legal outlets. The black market was the only source available, which brought blackmarket operations into a "gray zone" of beneficence halfway between criminality and anti-German subversive acts. Without it the budding resistance organizations could not have survived or functioned. In time, however, the distinction between resistance and the profit-motivated criminal aspects became clearer, though at almost all times there remained contacts of interest between the two.

Here and there among the very rich, the ruthless, the traitors, and the opportunists, there remained, like oxygen in water, minute islands of unconcerned and material plenty.

Not long after the first close brush with the Gestapo, several families of Pulika's *kumpania* were camping in a pleasantly secluded spot where a gravel road ended and sparse pine trees grew sturdier, near some grazing land with access to fresh running water. The women had the opportunity to do their accumulated laundry at the water's edge, somewhat down-stream from the camp. Nearby lay the monumental wreckage of a downed warplane, tilted up at one end, burned black, and grotesquely twisted out of shape. Its markings were still distinguishable. Around the torn edges of the metal and along its ripped rivet-dotted seams, it was embroidered with rust spots of sienna brown and orange. The landscape around it was ravaged by explosion, but already scarlet poppies were bursting forth. Naked, well-fed, dark-skinned little Gypsy boys clambered all over the wreck, invading its torn cavernous belly, exploring its bowels. They wondered at the intricacy of the defunct innards and laughed at the pitiful failure and demise of so powerful a machine. In the nearby meadow Pulika's skittish stallion pranced about. Its nostrils quivered as it snorted and the glistening lush brown skin rippled with little waves of pleasure. There were several chesty dapple-gray workhorses and a gelding. It had been a pleasantly warm and peaceful day.

Suddenly the dogs jumped up barking madly. We heard crunching footsteps on the gravel as the dogs ran forward to meet them halfway. A large group of uniformed red-faced Germans rushed toward the wagon camp. They were led by three civilians with a look of aggressive stupidity on their faces. It was obvious they had been drinking and we feared this was the end.

As the dogs snarled and barked at them hysterically, the soldiers kept moving forward undeterred. Out of the pack of maddened dogs, baying fiercely yet holding back, one bared its teeth. Without slowing his stride a noncommissioned officer pulled out an ungainly-looking service pistol and shot the dog point blank. The loudness of the report exploded upon my consciousness and shattered whatever remaining complacency I possessed. The body of the dog seemed to hesitate and then slowly crumple and go limp. The pack of yellow dogs scattered yelping. Women shrieked. The horses charged sideways or backtracked with stiffened legs, their heads high. They showed the whites of eyes widened by panic.

The German officer in charge regaled his cohort by subject-

ing the Gypsies to a torrent of abuse. Some of the Gypsies
squatting by the fire were kicked, but the physical violence
remained limited to that. The Germans had come to confiscate
horses, not to harm the Gypsies. It was apparently the furious
reception of the half-wild dogs that had exacerbated the
soldiers' latent aggressiveness. Several of the Germans made a
rapid selection from among our horses. They put halters on
them and took them away while the other soldiers and the
civilians terrorized the Gypsies and their families. They did
this with a strange mixture of the impersonal overfamiliarity
of the drunk and ill-disguised malevolence.

The Rom became silent and their faces clouded over. Their
expressions were soft and negative, their eyes deceptively
bland. For all their usual explosive intensity, they managed to
remain impressively unprovoked. Even though I was still very
young, and as such ebullient, I recognized, and perhaps reluctantly admired, the wisdom of not allowing themselves to be
goaded into desperate reacting. Under the circumstances this
only would have given the Germans an excuse for "justified"
violence. Deep inside my consciousness a mighty question was
formulating itself: how did one know when and how long to
hold back and when did it become imperative to hit out? Was
there not an inherent danger of ultimate self-conditioning and
an ever-receding threshold of tolerance until, indeed, it was
too late?

In the afternoon sunlight we watched the Germans march-
ing away with the self-conscious swagger of deeds well accom-
plished. Ahead of them the stolen horses trotted down the
road, their rumps rising and falling like receding waves.

When the Germans arrived, Kore, several young men, and
myself had been outside the camp limits. We had instinctively
hidden in the underbrush as it made no sense for us to walk
back into the trap. As we came out into the open my trousers
were torn in several places by the brambles. I was shaken by
my sense of guilty powerlessness. I seethed with a bitterness
which I resented and I felt a heretofore unsuspected longing

for death. To the Rom it seemed not overly dramatic. Once more they had had good luck in escaping a possibly worse fate.

They were exultant, celebrating the joy of being alive and free. What to me was a loss, to them was still a gain. What bothered me was not so much the appropriation—"requisition" as they called it, justified by vouchers payable "after the war"—of the horses, but the recognition that at all times we were at the mercy of potential despoilers.

With a mixture of loathing and exaltation I realized that the time of testing was over. I had to return to Paris to seek a full commitment. I had allowed time to slip by needlessly. I decided to act at once.

When the cooking was done, the fires were smothered and food was served even before the first star became visible against the darkening sky. I remember enviously watching Pulika eating with lusty appetite. The Rom had an unbelievable capacity for self-forgetfulness. They were making merry because they had survived.

That evening I told Pulika I intended to go see "him" in Paris. I still was ignorant of his name. Pulika said that he would convene the *kris.** Alluding to the Germans' vulnerability, even though they were at their zenith, he merely said that "no needle is sharp at both ends."

I intended to contact "him" in Paris and then hopefully join Pulika again in time for the gathering of the *kumpania* heads and be in a position to better evaluate the commitments of both sides. After a pleasant period of placid unconcern, abstraction, and inactivity I was forced back into the unenviable position of being the man in the middle, sharply aware again of considerations of racial sensibilities and wary of arriving at

---

* Within the world of the Rom, that strange phenomenon of a functioning anarchy, the *kris* (the council of elders who acted as judges), was the closest equivalent to a governing body. Under the present circumstances they alone could determine whether the Rom should undertake any concerted action against the Germans.

conditions amenable to both sides. Pulika advised me that a true dialogue was out of the question, but that I should be satisfied, as they would be, with some sort of coincidental monologue. He wanted to let Kore accompany me but it seemed too risky. I possessed a French identity card, demobilization papers, and such documents as would permit my moving about almost at will—until the day yet another supplementary document would be made indispensable.

As always Pulika seemed to be aware and well informed about newly developing patterns of illegal or anti-German activities. Pulika was gregarious enough by temperament to get his stimulation and satisfaction while at the same time achieving some practical purpose, talking with Rom and Gaje alike. When the occasion presented itself, he would not shy away from conversation with German soldiers. Pulika, it was true, was not readily identified as a Gypsy, which, officially at least, would have made him a socially undesirable contact. There were in our daily experience quite a few Germans who privately did not hew too close to the party line. Pulika liked to keep informed, to multiply and diversify his sources. Everything in his experience had prepared him for the role he was to assume. As he himself liked to put it, unlike the Gaje he had not "blunted his eyesight by reading print." He and several other Rom started taking a more active interest in the affairs of the world of the Gaje. At the risk of severe penalty, when he visited his Gaje contacts he eagerly joined them in surreptitiously listening to the broadcast of the BBC. These Gaje showed him what became known as "underground" literature, sometimes clumsily printed litho- or mimeographed tracts, leaflets, or posters. He would ask them to read these out to him, claiming he had "forgotten" his reading glasses to disguise the fact that he could not read. They shared and spread jokes of political, anti-German satire and of the newly relevant gallows humor.

The mad insidious hope for an invasion of British and Allied forces (then meaning Free French, Polish, Czech, Belgian, Dutch, and a few other governments in exile) slowly receded. As we were being starved, hunted, tortured and killed, the BBC merely broadcast the heroic increase of Britain's national industrial output for war.

There were increasing reports of isolated acts of subversion against the Germans which were assiduously passed on, embroidered upon, and exaggerated in extent and effectiveness. Endless ways were evolved to vex the Germans, which Pulika compared to something in itself no more affecting, yet effective, as the chafing of an ill-fitting collar or a small nail coming through the sole of a shoe.

At first we were unaware of being part of a spreading pattern of resistance that was to grow into an invisible but solid wall of systematic opposition which, if inventively multiplied, could in the long run wear down German morale. As the saying went, "even an ant casts a shadow."

Early the next morning Yojo and Kore rode out on some of the horses which, for obvious reasons, had been disqualified and rejected by the Germans. They were going on horseback to call together for the meeting of the *kris* the leaders of other traveling *kumpanias*. The date of the meeting had been set further ahead than would have been customary because of the difficulties and circumspection in avoiding the attention of the occupying forces. Besides making personal contacts, Yojo and Kore would leave *vurmi* to the same effect. Pulika told me they would meet at the previous winter's camping spot near a tavern whose owner was reliable and sympathetic. Zurka, the son of Pulika's dead brother Tshukurka, also went out to warn the Rom but chose to travel by himself on a newly acquired bicycle, bought from a woman whose husband was a prisoner of war and who apparently did not anticipate his imminent return. Traveling by bicycle made Zurka fairly inconspicuous among the masses of other bicycle riders, short of a raid and roadside barricades. Kore and Yojo on horseback had the advantage of being able to leave the open roads and travel crosscountry and over rough terrain, avoiding to a much greater extent contact with the Germans. Holding or riding horses in rural areas implied that one was connected with agriculture, a priority and therefore "protected" work category. Both modes of transportation had advantages and risks too.

Because of the requisition of our good horses the wagons had to be moved one at a time using the few horses we had left in a communal shuttle operation. We intended to illegally acquire new horses as soon as possible.

In the gray dawn Pulika drove me in the two-wheeled *taliga* to the railroad station some miles away from the camp. We waited outside the local cafe while the owner, a stout man in his late fifties with wild iron-gray hair and with whom the Rom had friendly dealings, finished sweeping the sidewalk in front of it. He briefly joined us at a table. According to the custom of the Rom, we had some brandy and sweet black coffee for breakfast. In this particular case both were excellent and strictly contraband. He left us occasionally to attend to his various morning chores. Suddenly Pulika gripped hard at my wrist in sign of affection. Then he let go as brusquely. I realized that this parting, every parting, could be our last. There was no point in pretending. We were faced by pitiless competent butchers and our chances of survival were tragically small. Pulika told me that whatever I decided to do I should do as a positive and virile choice, and to keep in mind always "that the greatest humiliation for a man was to have to prove his manhood."

CHAPTER FIVE

The city of Paris struck me as more movingly beautiful than I remembered; her people however looked more grim and shabby than I had expected. At first they seemed rude, sharp-tongued, gray, and unfriendly. The Seine looked glorious and the leaves were turning on the trees along the quays and gave them an air of sweet melancholy, a kind of end-of-vacation regret.

The German occupation was much in evidence everywhere with groups of healthy, sunburned, eager young soldiers on tours of the city. Everywhere also were swarms of clean-scrubbed, rosy-cheeked members of the female auxiliary forces who had a tendency toward overweight and whom the Parisians dubbed with condescending mockery "the gray mice" because of the color of their trim uniforms.

I was tempted to circulate through Paris to see the city, but instead I went straight to the convent on Boulevard Arago. The same nun opened the door. Unhesitatingly she let me into the hushed peace of the convent. Without showing any emotion she led the way down the long, cool, half-dark halls to the little room I had previously occupied. She opened the door and with dignified reserve she bowed me in without a word. The impersonal middle-class familiarity of the little room welcomed me back. The narrow iron bedstead and the wallpaper were evocative of a maidservant's room, with the very conventional clean white cotton bedspread, the varnished pitchpine dresser, the cheap mirror over the washstand with the old-fashioned flowered porcelain ewer and basin, the slightly musty odor and the crucifix over the doorway.

The memory of my first visit there intruded upon my mood.

Everything about it seemed dismal. I missed the sight and sound and the wildness of the Rom. I resented the apparent genteel sterility of the place and I waited for "him" with apprehension and irritation. There was something distressingly unreal and inappropriate about my having come back. In every respect it felt utterly unlike what I had expected it to be.

In my disarray and in anticipation of further disillusionment, I automatically repeated exactly my earlier acts in this same room. Unthinkingly, I washed my socks, underwear, and my only shirt. I washed my handkerchief and flattened it wet against the mirror, and again I furtively polished my shoes on the reverse side of the cotton bedspread. I felt ill at ease, lonely, and distressed. I had lost the sense of the reality and urgency of purpose for contacting "him." I lay with closed eyes on the bed and, only half awake, willed myself to dream about the Rom.

I awakened in the middle of a real dream in which a dog— the same dog, half-wild, yellow-haired, part wolf—choked in rage. When he barked no sound came forth. He lunged forward and a shot rang out loudly. The dog went limp in midair and in ridiculous slow motion landed on the ground spread-eagled and turned into some kind of fur rug. Then, as in a film, he would scramble up again, move in reverse, and suddenly start all over again: choke with impotent rage, lunge, and die in senseless repetition.

By the time a gentle hesitant knock at my door announced "him," I had found my bearings again and regained my composure. The dream had helped me focus. This time I had come to "resume our conversation," as he had referred to it when we parted, but on behalf of the Rom and their possible benefit rather than using them purely for his purpose and whomever he represented.

He looked drawn and, I thought, undernourished. His skin had acquired the quality of old ivory and I noticed he held his head slightly to the side. That and something in his gaze gave him a vaguely unpleasant appearance of distrust. Later I discovered it was due to encroaching deafness.

I had come directly from the rugged outdoor life of the Rom and, by city standards, I still had a tendency to speak loudly so that in the beginning of our second encounter he gently made me hush my tone of voice. Yet when I had managed to control my loudness I found he had difficulty understanding me because of his hearing. In contrast to the robustness and flamboyance of the Rom, he seemed brittle, shrunken, and gray. Gentle and reticent as he appeared to be, when he spoke he was incisive, precise, and direct in approach.

In answer to his questions, I told him about the forthcoming gathering of the Rom. He was sensitive enough not to display excessive curiosity as to when or where this was to take place. I told him about their willingness to cooperate within certain limits. After only ten minutes of spare but pertinent questions, the answers to which gave him as much of the situation as he cared or needed to understand, he outlined a course of immediate action. It was as if our last conversation had been only the day before; nothing had interrupted its sequence. More than ever, he fascinated me. I knew it was due to both his strange personality and his vision of effectively coordinated resistance. It was probably also partly the mystique of being close to the center of power and a feeling of gratitude for the existence of a pipeline to the outside, the naïve hope for directive and assistance in helping the Rom confront their destiny. Even though his vaguely distinguished mien had changed little, he seemed more abrupt and preoccupied. A trace of deafness seemed to make him more alert and suspicious. What he said clearly showed that he had given the matter a good deal of thought. He told me to scout around, select and form a cadre of willing determined young Gypsies who eventually could be given further specialized training, the nature of which he did not specify. He asked that as a first token of cooperation the Rom contribute part of their surplus ration cards (which they had plenty of anyway) and in other ways, at which they were adept, to help feed and provide for members of the illegal movement. The specific number and particulars would be transmitted by intermediaries as yet unknown to me.

He asked how the Rom felt about having small caliber firearms. He said he had been authorized by the "coordinating authority"—in our earlier meetings he had referred to "them" and "they"—to accord me special status. Once again he did not elaborate or deem it necessary to explain; maybe he assumed I knew more than I actually did or else he was building up a mystique for the work we were to perform (this occurred to me with a touch of Romany skepticism and impiety). It might be a way to abstract and protect the mysterious depersonalized powers that were to guide, even to dominate, our destinies; this was part of the sorcerer's folklore, a cryptic, intended confusion of substance and shadow. He did not condescend to explain the nature of the special status that had been conferred on me. He suggested that since the Rom derived a special joy from throwing the Gaje into confusion, they should be encouraged in the use of their cunning; they should be allowed to follow their particular bent—through their fortune-telling to stir up the oppressed and demoralized Gaje; to help change their attitude toward what they might otherwise come to accept as unalterable fate; to sow rumors; to plant specific predictions among the more personal aspects of their clients' palms, or in the cards, or by whatever other means they chose to use.

I had returned to Paris to submit the Rom's willingness to open a dialogue with the "coordinating authorities" through him, since it was obvious that the hierarchy, and everything else about it, was to remain conveniently anonymous. He volunteered that no doubt the Rom would legitimately need some sign beyond my simple word as go-between. He asked that the *kris,* or some other responsible inner circle, decide on a phrase of recognition which he in turn would transmit to the authorities. On a given day the message would be transmitted over a BBC broadcast from London, capital of the war, for all the Rom to hear as verbal confirmation of their mutual commitment. To avoid unnecessary complexities in transmission, the message should consist of only one simple sentence, yet it should be unconventional enough to be recognizable as exclusively ours, to serve as code, and verify his delegated authority.

From then on "they" would assure all my material needs. He said I would have to undergo intensive specialized training since I would function as part of his service, which, as he put it with an unexpected but gentle hint of mockery in his voice, was known in the polite understatement of official phraseology as "hazardous."

Before turning to purely technical matters he assured me that "they" were prepared to give the Rom a pledge of recognition of their wartime services according to their merit, which would possibly lead to a place in society after the war: job training or perhaps a general amnesty. Though I realized it was a bait, I was excited about the first, a place in society, interpreting it with youthful romanticism as the solution to racial prejudice. Their collaboration was the price they were to pay in advance for the blessing of a more just social condition and better status later.

He seemed curiously formal and I dimly sensed that the promises were kept general. For all their implied generosity they smacked of political expediency. Yet it was an ambitious promise which, as much as I could judge, he had been under no obligation to make. While I had no proof of this, it seemed an unnecessary lie. The mention of job training made me smile because I knew the Rom for what they were. But it was the mention of an amnesty—an amnesty for what?—that puzzled me most.

Since the Rom expected no long range assurance or promises—which when they came to be relevant were dismissed by "them" with a bored shrug as having been "not fully authorized," confirming our earlier suspicions—I did not pursue further. Pulika had emphasized that if we managed to survive, other things would take care of themselves and at the present "excess of sincerity could only lead us and them to more refined forms of lying."

After the auspicious statement of principle and aim by my mentor and superior in the service, I decided not to press the subject. There had followed a slight embarrassed pause during which I thought he silently thanked me with an indulgent half-smile. Possibly he was just reflecting on my vulnerable innocence rather than expressing relief at having completed an unfamiliar but required ritual.

When I had told the *kris* about these conversations, Bidshika simply said that to believe was a courtesy, not an obligation, and that after all only the blind and deaf were forced to believe. As far as immediate requirements were concerned, the Rom had been offered more than they, or for that matter I, had bargained for. Admittedly this benefited the "service" equally well. In regard to our formally undefined relations with the British, the Rom said "what did it matter what a blossom was called if it might not bear fruit" and "even wise men occasionally said foolish things, but only foolish men believed them." There was no doubt they believed that "even good seed could bring a bad harvest."

At that time even if I had been capable I might still not have dared face the reality of what would become of the Rom when they had outlived their usefulness. The Rom said that "the powerful stream does not refuse the small rivers" and added that "even the stream ends at the sea." With hindsight I was to realize that Pulika was deceived by no such illusions.

My superior, and only link to the hierarchy of the ephemeral "service," informed me of arrangements made for me for the following few days. I would be contacted, transported, and safely lodged. All I could do was allow myself to be guided, taught, and formed at their discretion. It was unreal. I could make contact with no one on my own; I knew no one, had no information, no leverage of any kind. Suddenly it seemed too unilateral for comfort. His rationalization, that the nature of our work made everything we knew potentially dangerous, offered no solace.

Then in seemingly contradictory show of confidence he invited me to have dinner with him. There was a touch of humor at the euphemism "dinner" in view of the severe war-time food shortage. As a second thought he specified *"chez des amis,"* at the house of friends. In the balmy summer late after-noon we walked through darkening streets toward the Latin Quarter. I tried to remember the way yet I instinctively forced myself not to look too obviously at the street names.

We entered a silent house with a gently decaying mildewed façade and shuttered windows. We climbed wide dark stairs spiraling around a center core where the typical Parisian elevator had once run. I had not noticed a concierge, under normal conditions a very conspicuous figure in the everyday life of the French capital. Through a skylight at the top of the stairwell came daylight faintly blue with dusk. There was a stale smell of garlic, cooked cabbage, and wet laundry.

We walked across a narrow terrace onto more steep narrow stairs and through a labyrinth of corridors. This part of the house had obviously been altered after its construction, subdivided to accommodate impoverished *petite bourgeoisie.* It was nostalgically reminiscent of an era of potted palms, cut glass, old lace, and genteel leisurely boredom. It was, how-ever, much in need of paint and badly ventilated.

The door was opened by a young man of powerful build. I was invited in and inadvertently learned my mentor's name, or at least his *nom de guerre,* when the young man, introduced as Jean-Paul, addressed him as Monsieur Henri.

I felt vaguely disappointed, yet I don't know what else I had expected to find. The furniture was covered by beige dust covers, "for the summer months," while the actual owner, away on vacation in the South of France, was absent. More evasions! In the entrance, under a portmanteau of deer antlers, stood an umbrella stand, a gleaming brass shellcasing of the 1914–18 war. From the other room we were joined by a man introduced as Robert. I was surprised to hear Monsieur Henri add in a seemingly casual matter-of-fact tone that he was the radio operator. They exchanged some remarks and we sat down around the partially cleared table. Jean-Paul brought plates, glasses, knives, bread, cheese, and a half bottle of red wine. While he poured the wine he slowly rotated the bottle between thumb and index finger as if he were serving some great *grand cru* wine. We were then served one warm dish which I found very bland compared to what I had become accustomed to among the Rom.

Robert seemed to be in his mid-thirties and he wore a wedding band. This discovery led me to inspect Monsieur Henri's hands and to my surprise I found that he wore one too. To judge by their language and manners, both Robert and Jean-Paul belonged to the working class. Their general attitude showed the unself-conscious assurance of skilled technicians who knew their craft. There was nothing unusual or secretive about them; on the contrary, they looked rather uninspired and average. But like Monsieur Henri their conversation always turned to the "occupation," as if they knew nothing else to talk about. At least Mr. H. had an intensity that could both frighten and inspire, and at times he became exalted. By contrast they seemed thoroughly levelheaded and practical. Theirs was an everyday business. Yet Robert was a practitioner of the occult art of secret codes and, as I was later to appreciate, courage to him was to remain seated while unemotionally operating his radio transmitting equipment.

The evening passed uneventfully, revealing nothing, adding nothing, and I was glad to go back to my solitary lodgings before curfew. I was picked up the following morning as prearranged, taken to another hiding place, and then on to basic training. I was taken to various places and, although I did not know Paris well, I had the distinct impression that I was being led by overly roundabout ways. I felt as if I were being passed from hand to hand like a ball. We had gone to a place in some grim working-class district. A fine rain had fallen continuously since daybreak. After a whispered exchange between my escort and my new host, I was taken inside and down humid stairs into an unusually large basement. The low vaulted ceiling was whitewashed and the rough-hewn wooden supports shoring up the ceiling made it resemble a mine or a petrified forest. Everywhere sandbags were piled high. Part of the basement was apparently used for training in the use of firearms. We passed the target-practice range, the armsmith's

workshop, a storage space where a young man was perfecting
his knife-throwing ability on a badly lacerated life-size manne-
quin in German uniform. Because I moved among the Germans, assuring the liaison between the Rom and H.Q. in
Paris, rather than being part of an action group or still further
afield in the secret army of the maquis, I was to receive only
the most elementary firearms training. To my chagrin, I would
not be allowed to carry arms. The risk was too great. In case
of a routine roundup by the German police my papers would
allow me to pass; being found in possession of a gun would
spell perdition, and in any case a gun would be fairly useless
in my particular circumstances. With youthful envy I eyed the
submachine guns and followed my guide. At the far end of the
basement—which, to judge by its vastness, must have extended below the street—I was handed over to a man who I
guessed must be my instructor. In the dim uneven light he
looked Oriental, possibly Indo-Chinese. He was small and
slight in build with a sallow complexion. He had dark black
hair and was in need of a haircut. He was dressed in what
looked like dirty pajamas. At first he seemed unimpressive and
taciturn, and I felt no particular emotion aside from a puzzled
indifference. He motioned me toward a thick, gray, soiled
mattresslike rug that covered the part of the area. I guessed he
must be some kind of boxing or wrestling instructor except
that his motionless left hand, frozen in an imitation of too
casual a gesture and concealed beneath a leather glove, revealed him to be an invalid.

Before the beginning of the war several of the Gypsy youth
and I had attended wrestling and boxing classes at local gyms
when several years in a row we had holed up for the winter
months near or in large cities. Having been exposed to more
athletic muscle-conscious gym workers and acrobats, I was
hardly impressed by my new instructor, who was called
Tonkin. I knew I could not hide from him the expression of
what I felt, or even a tinge of condescending commiseration
about his infirmity. The man who brought me to him remained
a few feet away watching.

Tonkin spoke little better than monosyllabic pidgin French

in a curiously whispered, rather high-pitched tone. After motioning me toward the mat he shuffled off his worn straw
slippers and joined me barefoot moving with small mincing
steps. Without any further introduction or preparation he sent
me sprawling, hurt, angry, and humiliated. I tried to suppress
showing any feeling except perhaps weary indignant surprise.
I got up and came up to him expecting some kind of explanation instead of which I was again violently thrown and pinned
down so that I really hurt. I no longer could suppress my
anger. I tried to reach and hurt him without any appreciable
result, only to be further brutalized. I was seething, but also
perhaps a little terrified at my unexpected vulnerability and
inability to retaliate. If he were to be my instructor—and he
was—there seemed no point in gratuitously hurting him, but
then again at that moment he was purposely hurting me for no
reason. This went on until I honestly believed he was simply a
sadistic fiend. I started wondering how I could get away from
him. Anger and hurt choked me and I wished I could have
killed him, even if this made no sense. The angrier and more
uncontrolled my thrusts at him the more easily he was able to
punish me more savagely, sidestepping or parrying my attacks
with surprising economy of effort. He suddenly stood still and
brought his one good hand palm forward facing me at shoulder height signifying that I should stop. And magically, hyp-
notized, I did. The other hand remained motionless at
stomach level. I remembered he was an invalid. He put his
hand on the back of my neck in an unexpected gesture of
affection. For a short instant his head was bowed as if in
prayer and there was no visible anger in him. Without condescension he addressed me as *"mon petit"* and said that he
would teach me to fight with the empty hand, as he called it.
He had wanted to know if there was violence in me. I had to
learn to curb my anger because it only blinded. I understood
the others' almost resentful deference to him. When it came to
fighting, he was obviously only an invalid in appearance.

A number of times I was subjected by him to the same
treatment and it was difficult not to become angry even when I
knew why I should not. I also learned from him that with such

a dangerous fighting technique (albeit barehanded), I should beware of using it in anger or too soon, but rather only if my life depended on it. Because, he said, I should not maim or kill where I only needed to hurt enough to compel restraint, for along with the technique I must learn the emotional restraint and maturity that should go with it. Yet he had no doubt there were in life occasions which warranted its full use. And, like him, I learned to bow my head after violence, as if in prayer or as a purification from the violent intent, in a nonreligious ritual of respect and love for life.

The days were full of intensive practical training and I discovered previously unsuspected, ever-new dimensions and layers of meaning and possibilities. But the nights seemed more lonely and dreary than I ever had known before. My companions were mostly easygoing, even nice in their own ways, but impersonal and interchangeable. It seemed as if even those capable of relating to others strenuously refrained from doing so. Each of us was isolated, surrounded by a zone of anonymous secrecy. We studied together and were taught the arts of subversion and of armed guerrilla warfare, but we never functioned as a group. There was a purposeful planned fragmentation, an intended lack or disruption of continuity and flow. Yet I was amazed at the organization all this activity must have required. The visible effect was that of a ghost train, functioning but without a conductor on board, without tender, stoker, or engineer. I was still being picked up and taken to the various sessions, but the locales kept changing even when the instructors did not. Also the couriers were rarely the same. Mr. H. was the only constant.

There were also sessions of a special kind of emotional learning. Drills to "practice" my assumed identity, background, and total personality, as I was told, "to avoid the incoherence of falsity." One day at dusk as I was leaving the building I was roughly shoved against the wall with the hard cold barrel of a gun pressed against my stomach. I had been unaware of the trap and angrily but belatedly cursed my lack of circumspection. Several men dragged me along in a viselike grip. They searched me in a needlessly rough way, scowling,

insulting, their remarks disparaging, their intent clearly antag-
onistic. They said they knew who I was in spite of the
documents in my possession "proving" my allegations. I was
bruised, bewildered, and bitter. They took turns interrogating
me—mock cajoling alternating with the most chillingly effective threats. I steadfastly maintained my cover story partly
because I did not know what else to do. I desperately resented
the humiliating circumstances I had fallen into and wondered
if I would simply vanish without a trace, without anybody ever
knowing what happened to me.

At this point Mr. H. walked in. In his controlled voice he
told them to leave and they did. It was a most unreal denouement. He looked wan and the blue of fatigue showed around
his eyes. He smiled his melancholy half-smile. The danger was
over and I suddenly felt on the verge of nausea. Mr. H. was
not my miraculous savior; he had simply decided that the test
of ability was over.

I was malleable clay to be formed and made useful or dis-
carded as waste. Obstinate and inconsistent, I resented being
open to their pressure and operable for their purpose. I
minded the perverse necessity that made all this mandatory. I
tried to comfort myself with the intimate knowledge that I had
not panicked and I was grateful for the years of exposure
spent with the Rom, which had no doubt helped prepare me
for such rude and ill treatment. But with commitment to the
cause—I had never before thought of it in such terms—I
should also expect confrontation. I could no longer speculate
about opposing the Germans from the safe vantage point of
theoretical abstractions. My vaguely motivated dream of social justice and political stability gradually receded; my pre-
occupation with ethics was replaced by the exigencies of my
new craft.

CHAPTER SIX

I returned to Pulika and the Rom in time to attend the meeting of the *kris,* but because I became impatient with the slow pace I frequently returned to Paris. Mr. H. allowed me, or even invited me, to participate in further "experiments" which in fact amounted to tests of my ability. I was goaded in this by a sense of mission, or of importance, not yet attainable for me in the planned activities with the Rom, who were slower to gather momentum than we had anticipated. The direction of this appeared at first less dramatically effective than I had dared dream. Mr. H. encouraged me to diversify my exposure to an ever-wider variegation of anti-German activities, tacitly implying that their indulgence was intended both as compensation and to assuage my impatience. Not heeding Pulika's warning that it was humiliating "for a man . . . to have to prove his manhood," I rationalized it instead as not wanting to waste any opportunity to oppose the enemy.

The first time I returned to Paris stands out as clearly in my mind as the first time I returned to the home of my parents after running away with the Gypsies at the age of twelve. Going away to the Gypsies and returning to my parents again (which went on for six years prior to the war) blended into one amorphous experience somehow blunted by repetition. So it was with my hovering between the world of the Rom, from which I was becoming increasingly disaffected, and the magnetic pull of Paris, which for lack of anything more direct was my private line to London and an immediate channeling for my energies, anger, general discontent, and lack of direction.

On my third return trip to Paris Pulika prevailed upon me to let Kore accompany me. At first he remained among the semisedentary Kalderash Gypsies living in the shantytown belt which at that time still circled the city. We had managed to obtain identity papers under the name of Iko, born in Tetuán de la Victoria, Spanish Morocco. This adequately explained his swarthy complexion. From this time on he made it a point to wear shoes, even though reluctantly and in the city only. He dispensed with the colorful kerchief around his neck, give-away of the true nomadic Rom, and completed his outfit with a riverboatman's cap, which had been dear to our young brother Putzina many years earlier. He assumed the traditional role of Joseph Tchouc-Tchouc, Arab rug peddler, an anachronistic but familiar figure in large prewar western European urban centers. Shortly after, both Zurka and Nanosh joined us and others were still to follow.

One late summer evening while turning a corner I was halted by several men in dark suits, arms at the ready. They barked at me, *"Stehen bleiben."* Suspecting another drill, I submitted to it with barely disguised irritation at what I strongly objected against as another and unnecessary repetition and exaggerated safety precaution. What seemed incongruous and even disturbing about the operation, however, was the number of people involved both as tormentors and as helpless prey. I objected impatiently saying I had been through all this before. Then they hit me in the mouth. They were really overdoing it even if they had to lend support to the fiction. And so I indignantly continued to defy them, to object strenuously, to be in every way intractable, even threatening to bring it to the attention of our superior. They let me go, bruised and indignant. Others were rounded up and taken into protective custody for further investigation at H.Q. in the Hôtel Letitia. Only belatedly did it dawn upon me that this had been the real thing—a German dragnet operation. By a miracle, I had passed.

Pulika had called together the Rom for a meeting of the *kris* at our winter quarters of the previous year, which was known to all of them. He had spread the word that in order to lessen the suspicion of the Germans and that of their local collaborators, the Rom should spread the rumor that they were gathering for the funeral of an important Gypsy figure. Symbolically tongue-in-cheek, this important man was referred to as *Bengesko Niamso,* Cursed German.

Pulika and a few Rom from our *kumpania* came with their wagons but most of the other Rom, all older and important men, contrary to tradition, came without their dependents in twos and threes by public transportation; a few came by horse-drawn *taliga,* still others came by pedicab, that replacement of the taxicab: a light, undignified-looking two-wheeled contraption pulled by a bicycle. Inevitably the gathering, however subdued, created a certain amount of amused curiosity. Some German soldiers stopped briefly to watch, but the Gypsy men's easy, dignified, unself-conscious manner allayed their initial suspicion. Nervousness attracts danger, the Rom said, and the reverse also held true. The absence of large numbers of Gypsy women and children made the assembly less provocative to the outside world.

Pulika and his *kumpania* had spent November and December, 1939, and January and part of February, 1940, in this place. Pulika, who was a royal spender, had gotten to know the owner of the Anytime Inn and knew he could rely on him. Pulika brought with him from the countryside half a slaughtered pig, a number of chickens and geese, bread, fruit, and vegetables, all unavailable in the city in those days of severe rationing. The fare was prepared at the inn with the help and supervision of the Gypsy women, as they had often done in the past. Pulika's wagon was parked nearby on a wasteland and served the other Rom as an indication, a *vurma,* of Romany presence. They called there first before being directed to the inn, which was closed for the day on the occasion of a private party, its shutters were drawn. The meal was abundant, as in the past, worthy of the gathering of the Rom and of Pulika's reputation.

The Rom ate and drank leisurely and exchanged news about those not present at the *kris.* It had been considered wise to limit both the invitations and the attendance. Old Bidshika made loud cha-cha-cha noises to bid the Rom be silent, and Pulika began the meeting of the *kris* with the traditional "By your leave, *Romale,* assembled men of consequence . . ." respecting the ritual complications of the Rom's code of courtesy. The Rom all knew each other and were either directly related or linked by an intricate network of personal loyalties and kinship ties. Yet during sessions of the *kris* they chose to speak in an abstract, proverbial, convoluted way to convey a direct statement. Their voices were subdued now and although their appearance remained casual as always, the unaffected dignity of their attitude revealed deference for the function they fulfilled as members of the *kris*. The Rom moved their chairs away from the tables at which they had been eating and drinking and sat in a wide half-circle, seemingly at random. After the boisterous feast preceding the meeting, a hushed solemnity heightened the importance of the moment. The very absence of ostentation of any kind emphasized the sense of drama. Over the years I had many times attended sittings of the *kris*. These took part in rural settings, often bucolic. That the present surroundings seemed an incongruous inappropriate background did not bother the Rom.

The inn had recently been remodeled in a badly integrated parvenu version of 1930s international modern style, all tubular chrome with olive-green leather upholstery. Indirect lighting set off, against the wall-size mirror behind it, the elaborate display of liquor bottles and brass sports trophies. The place smelled of newly laid linoleum and fresh varnish. The metal rolling blinds had been closed to keep out outsiders. The sun slashed through chinks, the artificial light looked sick. The patron-owner-bartender was busy behind a bar of majestic proportions, moving about glasses and bartending equipment. He was still fairly young and wore felt slippers, his hair carefully set in curls. The long sleeves of his stylishly striped shirt were pulled up from the wrists and held in place by elastic bands which outlined his biceps. A lone yellow canary whistled incessantly in its cage standing in the doorway to the kitchen. The kitchen had retained its old-fashioned red tile floor. The owner's mother-in-law attended the huge black castiron cooking stove or in turn listened to the news from a plywood cathedral radio. On the wall the family heirloom clock, swollen with ornaments, ticked obtrusively. It noisily chimed five minutes before and five minutes after the hour, as if to taunt the Rom in their sense of determined timelessness. In contrast to the decor, the assembled Rom seemed even more rugged outdoor people than they really were, athletic though heavyset. Their movements were controlled; even at rest they exuded pent-up strength and feline ease. Their dark eyes were alert, however, without seeming restless. Even indoors they wore their wide-brimmed black felt hats. They gave off a strong masculine odor of woodsmoke, horsehide, and per-spiration. The Rom knew the precariousness of their destiny under Nazi rule and the reason for their gathering here that day was clear to all of them.

Pulika said, "There is no reason to wait till the sun meets the moon. Even though we do not have all the facts about the Germans' intentions toward us, we must act now. Unlike the Gaje we are not burdened by their myth of objectivity. You have seen the mechanical rabbit at the race tracks which keeps moving just ahead of the dogs however hard they run. At harvest time it is too late to sow. The harvest is upon us. We know the Devil's own Germans (*l Niamsi le Bengeske*) hate the Jews and they hate everyone not of their race. From the fate of the other Rom caught up earlier in their dragnets we know there is no choice. There is no need for a further test of their intentions. Only the fish allow themselves to be caught twice by the same hook."

With a boisterous grin, Pani of the Tshurara, interjected, *"O shoshoy kaste si feri yek khiv sigo athadjol*—The rabbit which only has one hole soon is caught. So the time has come for the rabbit to hide, to run or to be eaten. To those of the Tshurara I propose we run without the benefit of the counsel of our peers. Aren't we giving new names to old troubles? Under the circumstances it is better to be at least a moving target."

With weary patience Pulika continued. "By your leave, again, *Romale,* assembled men of consequence, I propose that for now at least we forget about the rabbits, because in danger they are known to become insane with fear. . . ."

Pani took offense and glowered, but he was reminded by

the Rom that if he had something to say he should await his turn.

"Until now the Germans are still fighting against other enemies everywhere, and, partly as a matter of luck, we are still left alive. If the Germans win their war, if they conquer the world (*mukhenpe te khan la lumia*), they will hunt us down. As in the ritual of the hunt there will be no safety in hiding or running. The beaters will narrow down the sky and the earth and drive all toward just one open spot left: the spot where they can run to earth what they call the *Freiwild.*"

Pani could not let pass the opportunity to stagewhisper, "Back to the rabbits we have come." But nobody reacted to it.

"There is a time to pick up stones," said Pulika, "and there is a time to throw them too." After a slight pause—or was it a hesitation?—Pulika added, "If the trains do not run and if the trucks cannot pass . . ." Then, in the way of the Rom, he let it pass at that and sat down.

Old Bidshika stood up. He was still vigorous and clear-eyed despite his great age. He reached for a glass of wine on the table behind him and slowly poured out most of its contents. The liquid splashed on the floor where, instead of being absorbed by the earth as it would have in the open air where the Rom usually assembled, it made an ugly blotch on the immaculate linoleum. *"Te avel angla l Mule"*—In honor of the Ancestral Spirit, the Mule.

Symbolically inviting them to witness the proceedings about to take place, Old Bidshika addressed himself to "my father, my grandsire and forefathers all, and also those whose names we have neglected to remember . . ." addressing himself to both the dead and the living. He went on: "And you my peers, Lowara, Tshurara, Kalderash, kinsmen of all Gypsy races alike . . . *Gaje gaje si tai ame Rom sam.* The outsiders are only outsiders, but we must remember that we are the Rom. As at the time of the death of one of our own kind, we must draw together, we must lay aside all rivalries, all envy."

After this he added, *sotto voce,* the traditional protective formula used after mentioning the possibility of death. "May it [the omen] disappear like the darkness of night at the dawn.

We must forget all personal or intertribal enmity. As at the time of death we must humble ourselves and ask each other forgiveness for past offenses, in the ancient form of prayer, in ritual and mutual exchange of forgiveness, of the true Rom: *Te aves yertime mandar tay te yertil tut o Del*—I forgive you and may God forgive you too. We all know it is not right for a Rom to leave this life without having settled outstanding scores with those of his kind. No secret resentment or envy should remain unspoken."

Old Bidshika spoke and his was the voice of tradition. The Rom rumbled their assent. Like a sudden downpour on a sunny autumn day, there followed an emotional outburst of fraternal affection. They repeated to each other over and over again *"Te aves yertime mandar tay te yertil tut o Del."* They attempted to kiss each other's hands in a spirit of the humblest subjection, while each protested his indignation at the attention and in turn attempted to reciprocate the gesture. Many of the Rom were moved to tears reenacting a ritual parting at someone's deathbed. A young Rom rose slowly. He stood and waited, head bowed, until the commotion would subside, but the Rom were too deeply stirred to pay attention to him. The other Rom stood patiently aside and his behavior seemed strangely out of character. His deliberately undemonstrative stance implied that he, too, wanted to speak not in his own name, but with the authority conferred on him as a member of the *kris*. Although the Rom surrendered themselves with fervor to the ritual exchange of forgiveness and the emotion of deep friendship and at first were too deeply stirred to allow for distraction, he eventually won their attention by his quietness. His name was Kalia le Putzesko and he was known for his impetuousness and temper, but by his meek persistence he gained their interest as the noise subsided and one by one the Rom looked toward him, wondering what proposal he could possibly have to match the import of the ritual of forgiveness.

Kalia slowly removed his felt hat, suddenly revealing a shock of long black hair. He lifted his head as in a trance, his eyes fixed on an imaginary horizon far away. In a harsh imperious voice, painfully contrasting with everything that preceded and which for an instant made the Rom indignant about his arrogance, he said, "May my curse and the curse of the *kris* of the Rom precede and follow to the grave him who falls short of the obligations of kinship. Cursed be he who, even inadvertently, assists our enemies. May thunderbolts strike him. *Te malavel les i menkiva*—May the malignant disease waste him and may he melt away as the candle melts away. May the evil wind hit his midriff; may his liver rot inside of him; may the pieces of flesh fall away from his cursed bones; may God himself render him insane; may all the sticks and all the stones be used to hit him with; may God take away his strength and his pleasure; may he never be sated by food or his thirst slaked by drinking, nor warmed by any kind of fire; may he never find peace; may the worms eat him alive from the inside outward; may he no longer see the light of day; may he die among the Gaje without any dependents to close his eyes; may the Gaje bury him in a ditch like a dog; and may sterility wipe out his posterity."

A Rom took out his lighter. He struck the flint stone, ignited the long yellow wick, and gently blew the spark into a hesitant flame. Guessing his intent, two other Rom spontaneously reached for their folders of yellowish cigarette paper to improvise a symbolic torch. It flared up and they raised high the flame which they held in their joined cupped bare hands. It flared up and died almost instantaneously. The paper crinkled and turned into a delicate black ash which scattered as they let it go.

The Rom were standing up and loudly answered *"Bater"*— may it be so—to each damnation uttered, giving it magical power by their collective participation in the *Solakh* of the Rom, their most awesome oath.

Kalia's voice rose in pitch and he had to catch his breath. The enumeration of curses was profuse, imaginative, and chilling. Over and over again the Rom repeated *"Bater"*— may it be so—until it seemed their anger became exhausted. Luluvo mounted a nearby table and took over the litany from his younger brother Kalia to end it: "Not until the stone we cast into the water floats back to the surface of its own accord will we exorcise him, the *Mahrime,* the defiled one, who breaks our oath. *Rom Romestar, shav shavestar* . . . may our sons take revenge on his sons, and may the sons of our sons take revenge on their generation."

In the unwritten code of the Rom, excommunication, banishment from the tribe and from the Gypsies in general, was the harshest punishment that could be meted out. Under different circumstances a stone would have been symbolically cast into flowing water, but once more the fact that this could not be done did not seem to disturb anybody. There was a last, unanimous, loud *"Bater"*—may it be so—before the Rom started breaking up into small groups and fell to gossiping among themselves.

Yojo, Pulika's oldest married son, playing as usual at amused noninvolvement yet unobtrusively giving direction to what was about to turn into a chaotic hubbub, repeated Pulika's last cryptic phrase: "If the trains do not run and if the trucks cannot pass. . . ." As if he had waited for this cue, Pulika lifted his arms and asked to be heard. "It is no longer good enough," he said, "just to be foxes. We must now also learn to think according to the ways of the hounds."

Rising slowly, Dodo la Kejako said, "Forgive the interruption, father of my son-in-law to be. Without a spoon you burn your fingers, but I understand we have a spoon to share among us."

Pulika listened and smiled in turn before answering. "You travel faster along this road than I do, Dodo, but I come to the same waystations. On behalf of all the Rom we have been approached by the *Raya le Bare,** the big gentlemen. The *Raya le Bare* have made us an offer, which I, *Pulika le Yozhosko shav,* want to submit to the *kris.*"

"Those who bring should be made to feel welcome and heard out," a voice carefully commented.

Pulika went on. "In *Lowaritzka* we say that with good words you can sell even a bad horse. And because every road

* In Romani this term loosely covered any person in authority, as judges or high government officials.

has two directions I want your guidance and consent. I am aware that those who play out of need seldom win. The *Raya,* informed by their *Tshordane* [intelligence service], seem as aware as we are of the Germans' resolve to ultimately destroy us. The *Raya* have offered to help us whenever possible by warning us of imminent German raids. They offered us temporary shelter and hiding places, subsistence money, false identity papers, and, if we decide we want them, sidearms and explosives. But, as in all bargains, they expect something in return: the benefit of our experience and cunning, our commitment to oppose the common enemy."

"Even crumbs are bread," said someone, "and at least that which is given we won't have to steal." But a mocking voice from among the Tshurara objected with the sheer gall of that tribe: *"May mishto phabol o kasht o tshordano"*—stolen wood burns the better for being stolen.

Butsulo objected. "Pulika, do you ask us to forget all the wisdom taught us by our ancestors? I presume to remind you that violence is a self-defeating tactic. Does not pressure precipitate counter pressure? Could not the cure you suggest be worse than the disease? And the antidote taken before the poison turn to poison itself?"

Pulika replied, "I know that those who are to hang will never drown—but I would rather live. As we live as Rom, we also die as Rom. *I tshatski tsinuda de tehara, vai de haino, khal tut*—The true nettle stings from the beginning. But we must remember that the teeth outlast the tongue, and the flexible the rigid. To be effective, the benefits of resistance must outweigh the penalty. I know you are all men of proven courage and wisdom. Not all delay stems from cowardice and I know that those who are forced to go to church pray badly. All I hope to gain from you is a pledge of trust, and from those who share my sense of urgency to cope with a new and perhaps more terrible unknown, I ask only an informed consent. I want to inform the *kris* that I have decided to explore the *Raya*'s offer, to use the spoon extended. If worse comes to worst, to keep alive against the odds. I see no evil in casting our lot with that of the Gaje. At least let us try to use them."

Some Tshurara kept scoffing under their breath. They were becoming restless and unruly, like children whose attention span was strained by too long a school period. One Gunari mumbled about making a dog for the sake of a bone. Another one commented derisively about the need for any kind of outside assistance: *"Te avel mange bakht drago mange wi te avav po gunoy*—All we need is good luck. With luck I would not even mind sitting on a dunghill."

Old Bidshika objected. "If you touch honey, you will be forced to lick your fingers afterward."

I was impatient. My personal commitment to the Resistance was still wavering. Tinged with romanticism, I had dreamed of making the Rom fierce again, to try to make them assume virtues—or could they be defects?—they did not possess. In vain I tried to gauge the substance from the shadow, the reality behind the appearance. This meeting of the *kris* was maddening. It was obviously about to end inconclusively. Pulika listened to them and smiled. He seemed well satisfied with the Rom's skepticism. He had informed the Rom of his dealings with the *Raya* and, since there had been no real opposition to it, he knew he had their tacit consent to pursue it. The young and more restless Rom got up and pressed forward.

Summing up the situation, as if it were for himself, Bidshika said, "Where the needle goes, surely the thread will follow—*Kay jala i suv shay jala wi o thav*. As for the others, let them exercise their right of dissent. No one sins for someone else, and every sin has its own excuse." Bidshika held up his left hand, fingers spread out, and his gesture was understood by all the Rom to signify the harmony of differences.

In the hall there was a thickening blue cloud of tobacco smoke and the smell of perspiration was pungent. There followed some ceremonial expressions of good will, then the Rom departed with a loud *"Zhan le Devlesa tai sastimasa*— Go with God and in good health."

Many of the Rom wanted to travel back to their own encampments before curfew time and some had far to go. A few men remained and Pulika called for a round of drinks.

Soon the Rom returned to the subject of the *kris*. Possibly to appear wise, Kalia, who was known as a hothead, said, much out of character, "The loaded gun frightens the one at whom it is pointed, but the unloaded gun frightens both him and the one who holds it. Is it not, after all, the Gaje's war? The *Raya,* our would-be benefactors, are after all only Gaje, and all dogs dream only of bones. *Gaje gajensa, Rom Romensa*—The outsiders with the outsiders, the Rom with the Rom."

Yojo answered, *"Piri telemosa tshi athadjol o kam*—The kettle that lies face down cannot catch much sunlight. To survive, and only when talking to them in their own language, we should remember that if the *Raya* say apples grow on an oak tree, we should believe them. We should believe them and say yes to them. But not to death!"

As the time of curfew approached the Rom left the tavern and walked back to Pulika's wagon. Kore noted that none of us appeared particularly sad after the wake for the apocryphal Mr. Niamso. The Rom suddenly remembered that the excuse they had given for their gathering here was a burial. Would this arouse suspicion? The Rom laughed boisterously and, playing the part of the Gaje, said, "With those unpredictable Gypsies you never know what to expect."

The night was clear, cool and peaceful. Clouds of mosquitoes filled the air as we sat together smoking quietly in leisurely enjoyment of simple pleasures. The Rom asked the small children to light their cigarettes for them at the softly glowing embers left from the daytime fires. An infant wailed nearby and the young *bori* (literally daughter-in-law, but freely used to designate any young woman) were quick to attend to its needs. The late midday meal preceding the *kris* had been copious and we stilled our hunger that night with a simple but well-seasoned meat-and-onion hash. I noticed that Pulika nodded at what the Rom were saying without really listening. Nearby were the dark shuttered houses of the Gaje.

Before going to sleep I went with Pulika to look at the horses. I shared my *dunha,* sleeping eiderdown, with several Rom guests.

The *kris* had met and a precedent was established. As the Rom said, *"Kai jal o vurdon vurma mekela"*—Where the wagon goes a trace is left. Yet I felt no particular sense of joy, only one of exasperating emptiness. I was strangely disappointed because it had been so unimaginably different from what I had expected. I felt I was drifting still further away from the Rom.

"O zalzaro khal peski piri—Acid corrodes its own container," said Pulika, seemingly apropos of nothing, but reading my mood with uncanny empathy. "Fear not death, but life. What makes stealing evil is the greed in it, more than the taking, and beware of lust in the killing. Beware of romantics gone awry who believe they have to use violence and deception. Beware of experience without wisdom. If we Rom have a tradition of dissent, it is only for selfish reasons, beyond political or military necessities. The forest is burned by its own wood. And the stallion that is fed too many oats only becomes unmanageable. . . ."

Then Pulika lay down and let the noises of the night take over.

I awakened very late the next morning to the typical rapid firing of a German submachine gun, guttural shouts of *"Achtung,"* and much running about. After the first instant of panic I realized we were not the immediate target of the commotion. German soldiers came running from several directions excitedly pointing at the sky. More shooting followed. The first obvious thought was of Allied parachutists or pilots bailing out—but not in broad daylight. It turned out to be nothing more dangerous or offensive than a happy kite floating triumphantly high in the sky. In those days even flying kites was *verboten*.

There followed similar gatherings of the Rom in many places, spreading essentially the same message, confirming, repeating, consolidating, and developing.

I was grateful for Pulika's open participation, which he had not heretofore indicated to me as his intention, and for his willingness to take full responsibility. I spent a few days with the family before my irrepressible restlessness drove me back to Paris, hungry for action.

In their own individual ways, Kore, Zurka, and Nanosh were becoming as fascinated and involved in training as I had been earlier. Kore and I drew together increasingly and were to grow closer still, while somehow Zurka and Nanosh gradually became more estranged from us. I was too involved in learning and doing things to stop and wonder if these were the doings of Mr. H. and if so why, though I knew full well that, to say the least, it would be difficult for him, or anyone else for that matter, to establish a secondary reserve liaison in case I came to grief.

Later on Mr. H. had said in reply to my impatience for more meaningful action against the Germans, "At this early stage 'specialists' would feel wasted." In awe I had dreamed of, and maybe also dreaded, the promised "specialists." I also wondered what superhuman qualifications were required to graduate to specialist.

At the beginning of the following month Kore came back to Paris to deliver to Mr. H., whom only I knew how and where to reach, the Rom's first token contribution of several hundred sheets of ration stamps valid for the month ahead. These were to be used by the organization to feed and support their members in hiding.

By this time I no longer lived at the convent but only used that address to contact Mr. H. Whenever the necessity arose, I would move in for a day or a night and wait until he got in touch with me. Remembering the miserly meal I had shared with him and the radio operators and which I had thought excessively frugal, I tried to say to him that I hoped he would help himself to his share. I said this without intending to criticize his hospitality or his diet and I hoped without appearing indiscreet or rude. He looked at me amazed and reproving. He sternly said one should not expect laxity from those who render essential services. When I left he said simply, "Take care of yourself," showing a concern for my personal welfare he had rarely indulged in before, perhaps to soften his earlier severity even though it had not been directed at me personally. As I hesitated, not quite sure of what he meant (or maybe I was just surprised at his unexpected solicitude), he added, "Because some operatives do not return."

I closed the door and stood outside, suddenly cut off, at the mercy of intrusive afterthoughts I was sure he had no intention of calling forth. He had probably just intended it as a friendly warning. I turned off the flow of self-destructive fantasies and walked away into the waiting night.

CHAPTER SEVEN

By force of circumstance, their particular predisposition, and their mode of life, the Rom had sooner or later, and practically without exception, come in contact with elements of the Resistance or become involved in some aspect of anti-German activities. They had done this independent of either Pulika or me. I was told by Koka la Helako how one day, shortly before dusk, he had noticed a distraught, disheveled, haggard creature at the edge of the woods. Koka had pretended not to notice him while his young and beautiful wife Hela had motioned to the fugitive and, after coaxing him into submissive immobility, had slowly approached him. Only then did Koka join them. First they fed him, after which he spilled out his concern not in the first place for himself, as they anticipated, but for a companion dying of fever somewhere back in the forest. There were not just the two of them, but a whole band hiding away. They had some weapons between them, he had said, but they had become unaccountably cut off from the outside world. One day the courier had not come. Days had passed and now one of the men was dying and they did not know what to do or how or where to reach a doctor. The man's story seemed obviously true and after some deliberation Koka had ventured with him into the forest. Hela stayed behind with the children. So as not to allow for any untoward surprises, they agreed that if anyone showed up they would hide in the underbrush until Koka returned. If he found the camp deserted he would whistle the special Lowara whistle or, better still, before reaching the encampment he would imitate the cry of the cuckoo. Deep in the forest Koka found a shockingly primitive shelter, full of raw and desperate men. There was a mood of fear, distrust, and hatred, yet the men displayed a curiously innocent carelessness about the most elementary safety precautions. Everywhere were piles of trash and an abundance of scattered human excrement at the immediate periphery of their living area. Aside from their totally inadequate organization for survival, they appeared in urgent need of everything. Thrown together by happenstance, they survived in continuous fear of starvation. Koka suspected that the wounded man must have been hurt by carelessness with firearms. For lack of adequate medical attention, the wound had become infected and had slowly festered. The man was incoherent, shivering with fever, dazed with pain, silent, half mad, and catching his breath in painful racking sobs. They did not dare to call a doctor lest it awaken the suspicion of the Germans stationed at nearby villages, yet they feared for him the horror of a senseless death, and for themselves haunting self-reproach and guilt.

Late that night Koka went on horseback to seek a country doctor several villages away. He was accompanied by one of his small children and he insistently begged the doctor to come with him to attend to his wife, who was about to give birth. They must hurry back, said Koka, because he had been forced to leave her alone with their other small children. The alibi might also serve the doctor himself. Koka helped him harness his horse and hitch it onto the carriage. Reluctantly the doctor had followed the Gypsy into the night. At the Gypsy encampment, Koka revealed the truth to the disgruntled doctor, whose old-fashioned patriotism made him unexpectedly thank the Gypsy for his intercession. When they reached the camp deep in the forest it was already too late to save the wounded man.

When we happened to be in the region a short time later, Koka took Kore and me to "his" hidden camp. We traveled by wagon through a scarcely populated region of scattered homesteads. Young peasant women were driving the livestock home for the night from the pastures. They had an air of mannish independence and pretended to be unaware of our presence. Descending twilight already began to blue the horizon and we inhaled the serenity of dusk. We penetrated the very still fragrant pinewoods, at the edge of which we set up camp for the night. I felt strangely safe in the stillness of the premature sylvan nightfall. That night we supped on a rich bean soup. The following day we went into the forest carrying provisions and tobacco, but for quite some time we found no sign of human presence, no distant sounds, no smells of cooking or of fires. The abundant insect life only seemed to emphasize their absence. When we finally found the location of the camp it was deserted and had been destroyed. The unusually loud droning of blue-black flies everywhere by the great fallen trees, against which the makeshift shacks had been built, uncannily warned us of disaster. On the way Koka had told Kore and me about the fugitives and he displayed an indulgent superiority when he spoke of the evidence he had seen of the Gaje's frailties. He remembered their perennial groping about for food.

The great trees were pockmarked by bullets. The rain-bleached shacks with the leaky roofs were collapsed, showing the wood sides weathered raw and rotting. And all about us were the humiliating evidences of decaying human matter contrasted by the gentler decay of leather straps and boots. There was a sickly bittersweet stench. Involuntarily we inhaled deeper than we meant the breath of overripeness. How deceptive had been the appearance of quiet and peace. The men had been butchered.

We left the provisions and the tobacco we had brought, as an offering to the dead, these tragic marginalia of war, and by extension to all such who had died and were still to die.

We left the forest in haste, Koka and his dependents to resume their wartime wanderings from village to village. Kore and I were impelled to surrender ourselves more fully to the exigencies of our new inescapable functions, which, admittedly, spelled an accelerating collision course. Justifying it, Kore said, *"Nashti jas vorta po drom o bango"*—You cannot walk straight when the road is crooked.

The Rom often ran into groups of fugitives trying to survive in the woods or hills and who in many cases could not have been worse prepared for it. They came to escape and to hide from the Germans, but also with the intent of actively opposing the enemy in paramilitary actions. The Rom wondered not only if these people would manage to survive the winter, but also at the staggering folly of their impatience. But amidst vast confusion a vast reservoir of potential guerrilla fighters slowly emerged. Many of these men had had no choice; others had been driven by truly patriotic and anti-German feeling. What eventually became known as the Resistance in the majority of cases started independently and in complete isolation. Small groups of men went to hide in the woods as purely defensive emergency solutions to individual security problems—to avoid deportation as slave labor, separation from loved ones, captivity, or even destruction depending on the vagaries of individual identity and personal history. Some went into hiding (often in cleverly thought out, adequately planned retreats) and remained isolated for the entire duration of the war, emerging only after the liberation. For others, saving themselves and fighting the enemy meant escape to Sweden, Switzerland, Turkey, or Spain in order to join Allied forces. Quite a few did; many more tried. Some who reached England returned to their occupied homeland after thorough and specialized training, dropping from the skies on moonless nights to direct, train, and coordinate resistance groups. They came to establish radio contact with faraway invasion headquarters in London for the western theater and with Cairo for the southeast of Europe, to both of which they regularly transmitted coded reports.

Perhaps because of accidents of timing and a providential play of circumstances, combined with the interaction of Monsieur Henri and the Rom, I had occasion to become part of the "underground." I was exposed to a wealth of seemingly inconsequential details, learning that truth was rather more complex than fiction. Involved with the movement both at the very bottom and also at the top, I saw the Resistance emerge piecemeal and chaotically before it progressively broke up into specialized sections of activity.

Being wholly surrounded by enemies and operating under every conceivable disadvantage complicated recruiting and aggravated the administrative difficulties inherent in overall organization on a regional, and later on a national, scale—to coordinate this armed struggle with long-range efforts of the Allied liberation H.Q. in England; to fit their action into overall strategy. Without outside assistance, most of the units were woefully underequipped.

Before a more rigid hierarchy came into being there were numerous quasi-independent resistance groups. Often these were small commando units of hardened, determined, sometimes undisciplined men with an essentially terrorist approach —they roved across the lands, "like Gypsies," to avoid localizing the conflict.

Though it was clearly too early for open fighting, men of military age would continue to drop out of sight over a period of years and by roundabout ways seep into the general reservoir of manpower. Outside life went on with most households deprived of fathers, husbands, and growing sons, as many of these upon reaching manhood opted to join their elders in the underground rather than wait to be drafted by the Germans for labor in their war industry. Months and then years went by without much apparently happening. In the beginning they had said "if still necessary by spring," but then after having somehow survived the long hard winter they spoke of "next fall. . . ."

After the Nazis attacked the U.S.S.R. the Resistance inevitably polarized into right and left wings in the midst of intrigues and susceptibilities which vastly complicated our already difficult plight.

Among those who could afford to openly function within the German-controlled order, many were keeping records "for the day of vengeance." Protected behind legally blameless exteriors, they were driven by an urge to bear witness. These "statisticians" kept assiduous but unobtrusive surveillance, suppressing for the while all evidence of rightful indignation. There were those who kept our records but who, to assure our safety, in every other way remained outside illegality. Still others worked alongside the enemy and kept the underground informed. Some who worked for the Germans sought delayed political salvation, betting both sides, while others were blackmailed into it by family considerations.

Numerous organizations emerged to cope with specific situations, some consisting of just a few close friends, providing hiding places for the rare surviving political suspects or Jews. Some limited their humanitarian objectives exclusively to rescuing Jewish children from the hands of criminals. Separated from their parents, these children were "adopted" by non-Jewish families who brought them up as their own. On a larger scale and coping with larger numbers, they were placed in the safety of a boarding school or in Catholic convents, obscuring the nature of their origin.

Because of the secrecy in which all these activities took place, the groups were unconnected, fragmented in endless individual parts, often duplicating and overlapping each other's efforts, or leaving wide open otherwise unexplainable gaps. Constant harassment and interference by German agencies of repression further disrupted the continuity of operations. There were the local "reception committees" which coordinated Allied air drops of war matériel, who checked cover stories and cleared parachuted agents for security. Other committees "cleared" Allied pilots shot down over German-held territory after they had been "collected" by agents of the specific retrieval areas in which they had landed. Once fully "processed," they were transferred to efficient, wide-ranging, and complex escape routes. There were also satellite "maintenance organizations" with limited objectives and of a specialized nature.

There was a perennial need for establishing contacts and scouting for expertise, often of an unusual and highly specialized nature, as counterfeiters for the manufacture of documents or safecrackers and burglars.

As part of a vast psychological warfare effort there were numerous independent clandestine printing presses producing handbills, leaflets, posters, and occasionally even books, notably *Les Éditions de Minuit*.

There were also the euphemistically named "action groups," or death squads, which summarily executed proved or suspected traitors to the cause. These self-styled enforcers of justice sprang up spontaneously in different districts. The details of their actions became grimly familiar: found on a lonely country road, far enough from any inhabited spot to minimize reprisals by the enemy, though as a rule the Gestapo liked betrayals but despised the traitors. Some of the victims had their hands tied behind their backs, others had been tortured and were mutilated for warning or revenge. The rationale was to avenge the dead of the Resistance, but there was little doubt that for some there may have been a more personal motivation. Where did political terror end and sheer banditry begin? There were agonizing arguments about defaulting allies whose wavering opportunism seriously endangered the movement, or incorrigible village gossips, or sometimes even vociferous patriots who knew too much and talked too loudly. The inevitable arguments were "if we do not do this (or that) we shall lose the war," and at times the choice truly did appear to be only between murder and suicide. And intermittently terror reigned and executions were frequent as murder and arson alternated between their side and ours like an insensate morbid game of checkers played *ad absurdum;* our move, their move; and it seemed increasingly motivated by vindictiveness alone. Little by little a normal sense of compassion became atrophied in a desperate need for survival. We learned that crime could be a mere matter of definition.

Since the requisitions by the Germans of some of our horses, Pulika and the members of our *kumpania* shared those that were left. The wagons had to be moved one by one using the same team of horses all the time. We no longer rode in the wagons but walked beside them. In badly rutted dirt tracks we all helped push to spare the horses as much as we could. We traveled shorter distances and remained mostly in remote rural areas. As the general war situation gradually became more tense, Pulika advised that we leave behind some of the wagons in secluded spots under the "protection" of well meaning Gaje friends or business contacts, just as in normal times we would have chosen winter quarters where part of the families stayed on while those who provided for them went out on quick forays.

Aside from the lack of horses, smaller numbers of wagons on the road would attract less attention. The varnished heavy oak wagons typical of our Gypsies were abandoned in favor of the less conspicuous covered farmwagon still used by the peasants. The Rom abstained from wearing overly bold or loud colors. The women wore frayed overcoats or raincoats over their long dresses, and they no longer wore the elaborate solid-gold necklaces, bracelets, and earrings they used to wear before the war. The most they dared were small golden rings through the earlobe as affected by the local peasant women on special occasions. The Gypsy women, however, could not restrain themselves and wore these every day. I noticed one day that Pulika's fierce drooping mustache seemed more conservatively trimmed than I could remember ever having seen before. His hair, and that of most of the men, had been cut, though it was still full and long by accepted local standards. Pulika and the responsible men of the tribe restrained the others from ostentatious behavior, from the more usual mischief as practiced by the Gypsies under other circumstances, and anything liable to draw the attention or latent hostility of outsiders.

Sometime before, Pulika had illegally transported a man as a favor to a local innkeeper, and in time we had transported many more. They had gone underground and we now were engaged in transporting crates for them, frequently shuttling in and out of forests and deserted places, which as Gypsies we could do fairly easily without arousing undue suspicion. The crates contained explosives and guns. We brought the partisans news from the BBC, for which men living in the isolation of the woods were hungry. Gypsy women and their children frequently went into the woods "to gather herbs," reducing the general insufficiency of communications. Admittedly the Rom were interested in "establishing credit" and so one day Pulika decided to try out their hospitality. We spent several days in the semidarkness of the great forest abounding with wildlife, not far from a somber-looking rather dilapidated hunting lodge which had become a G.H.Q. of sorts.

Pulika's friend, as we had become accustomed to calling

him, welcomed us warmly. He was a solidly built, middle-aged man with a dark square mustache and light short hair, dressed in a loose well-cut corduroy hunting suit. I remember fleetingly admiring the dark brass buttons alternating boar's head and stag's. Surrounded by his men he seemed a *bon vivant* and he stood out by his aristocratic self-assurance, which I later found tempered by a measure of emotional detachment. It seemed that he had taken a strong personal liking for Pulika in past dealings with him in which I had had no part, and because of Pulika he had become partial to the Gypsies as a whole. After the crates were unloaded, inspected, and stored away, we were invited to eat with our hosts. But when Pulika discovered that the evening meal consisted of game he declined for all of us, saying we had already eaten. In view of our many hours traveling through the woods, this seemed unlikely, but nothing more was said. At that time the Rom still observed the strict traditional taboo against eating game because "it is free and wild like ourselves."

Pulika's friend, known by the somewhat unlikely *nom de guerre* of *le Capitaine* Lothar (simply *le Capitaine* to his men) and *le Chef* to his intimates, was a man of unquestioned authority and seemed much at ease in an atmosphere of masculine camaraderie. Most of the group were back-country men familiar with life in the woods. His "adjutants" were city people, but sportsmen used to the outdoors. The gathering was distinctively reminiscent of a hunting meet on the eve of a *grande battue*. I had the facetious impression that for the occasion even the local poacher was allowed to be part of the family affair. For all we knew, le Capitaine was a local squire who had decided to go underground on his own estate. Yojo, Kore, and several of our men remained with the women and children in our wagon camp a few hundred yards from the bivouac, while I accompanied Pulika to the hunting lodge where we spent several hours with le Capitaine and his inner circle. Everybody called the camp *"les marcassins"* (the wild boars), which we surmised may have been the original name of the lodge or possibly the game inhabiting the forest. Like a redoubt, the lodge was built from boulders and heavy timber.

It had a huge stone fireplace which, for obvious reasons, was not in use. To save on fuel it was lit by a single storm lamp. Everywhere were folding metal fieldbeds, stacked up sleeping bags, and much camping gear. In a corner next to the heavier armament stood some prize double-barrel hunting guns with gleaming walnut stocks. Pulika looked at them with admiration and, invited to do so by le Chef, he picked one and handled it with the expert casual ease of a connoisseur, which somehow I had not expected from him as a Rom.

Les marcassins, as they liked to refer to themselves, brewed excellent coffee, which in the evening they served with sweet condensed milk. Everything about the camp reflected a miracle of foresight, which le Chef shrugged off engagingly as *"un impromptu fait à loisir."* Yet I could not help wondering at his casual trust in us and his essential dilettantism. In the evening they also distributed the day's small ration of hard liquor. Smoking was allowed indoors. We sat in a wide circle with the storm lamp casting a harsh light as focal point.

Le Chef was a lively raconteur and proved to be as rewarding a listener to Pulika's Gypsy stories. In spite of his *nom de guerre,* he spoke with cavalier confidence about himself, too exulting to be careful, too trusting to care if through his unguarded stories he might be tentatively identified. Even when the display of unreserved trust and familiarity was flattering, I could not help but wish that he would feel the need to be just a little bit more careful. We learned that he was a lawyer by training, though obviously of independent means, and had been for a time director of an international news agency. He was well connected in publishing and he had traveled extensively. He had spent much time in the region and knew it well. Our supposition was soon to be confirmed; he was the owner of an "estate," in fact, with the exception of his adjutants (who formed a close group of relatives, intimate friends, former hunting companions, and summer guests), most of the other men were in one way or another in his employ and their families received compensation, from "private sources" he had said, for their continued military service. Under the circumstances, they constituted a small-scale pri-

vate army. He and his friends lived in the lodge, whereas the
men lived in army tents and used roofless showerbaths and
latrines built from stakes driven in the ground. The staff
carried sidearms at all times. With an air of heroic fantasy
they spent much of their time earnestly studying detailed
military topographical maps, surrounded by the theatrical
paraphernalia of field glasses, compasses, and sextants. Despite their rusticity, they managed to retain an air of patrician
prosperity.

Le Chef was unvaryingly even-tempered and jovial, spending his days and part of his nights inspecting, checking,
encouraging, or reading—as I recall, Xenophon's *Anabasis,*
and *The Frogs* by Aristophanes. During the time we spent
among the *marcassins,* he visited us regularly and seemed to
derive a special pleasure from fraternizing with "his" Gypsies,
quite possibly it occurred to me, like the urban sophisticate in
search of the regenerating primitive. He squatted like the
Rom, drank our sweet black coffee, and shared our food. Yet
independent of our relationship to him, our contact with his
men remained purely pragmatic and only somewhat cordial.

The vast dusky forest of tall pines was hauntingly beautiful,
yet we were forever conscious of the danger of accidental
forest fires. The summer and fall had been unusually hot and
dry, until, to our relief, it rained almost continuously for
several days. It filled the air with rushing sounds and the thick
carpet of pine needles underfoot became spongy and smelled
more strongly of mold and fungus, almost overwhelming the
pungent fragrance of pine resin. Overhead the swaying timber
moaned, sighed, and swished in the wind, accentuating the
hushed resonance below.

The downpour slowed to a steady drizzle. When at rare
intervals the rain momentarily stopped, we heard heavy rain-
drops seeping down from the water-laden pine needles of the
treetop canopy to the small pools gathering at the roots where
they formed silver air bubbles. Everything was wet, soggy, and
warm. The heavy humid air became oppressive to breathe and
formed a dusky mist before our eyes. Within hours it brought

forth abundant fungi and molds, flaccid, yielding, spreading, iridescent toadstools, many-hued mushrooms, fascinating and repugnant, threatening like some unknown mortal disease. A few were edible but most were deadly poisonous. To le Chef and his epicures they were an avidly sought-after delicacy, an occasion to celebrate by opening of a bottle of rare wine *"de derrière les fagots,"* reserved for extra-special occasions. To the Rom, mushrooms were an unmitigated abomination and the simple thought of anybody eating them kept them away from the hunting lodge for days.

Everything was sodden and dripping. At night we slept in moist damp bedding. At sundown one day the sun broke through the dull overcast skies and, like a promise, soon filled our damp monochromatic environment with diaphanous amber light which before the night turned to amethyst. After the rain the air was full of flying ants, moths, and mosquitoes. We lived in the inaccessible vastness of the forest and the restricted field of vision of the dense growth gave our hiding place the protective and confining appearance of a great cave. The outside world ceased to exist and we lost the awareness of being threatened. But as time passed I felt more and more like a prisoner.

Before the break of dawn one day I awakened at the sudden report of a distant gunshot followed by its echoing repercussions. After an infinitesimal pause the stillness of the shadowy forest was broken again. Wary of annihilation, I was taut for action. I felt like a cornered animal. Calling my name in a soft halting voice, Keja brought me to my senses, recalling what le Chef had warned us the preceding evening. It had sounded quite improbable. The Germans, who had requisitioned and lived at *"le Château"* (which we understood belonged to le Chef), had invited some important military guests to a formal hunt—*"Treibjagd"* they had called it. I strained my ears to the baying and excited yapping of the dogs. There followed more shots and the sounds of headlong crashing in the underbrush. By now birds arose in screaming protest all over the forest. Throughout the day the reports of rifles and shotguns echoed through the timber stands.

It was said that with the Germans' tacit knowledge le Chef had been forewarned and that an accommodation had been reached between them to avoid "unpleasantness"; the German gentlemen were themselves not a little caste conscious. Outwardly unconcerned, le Chef came for his usual early morning "inspection"—as he persisted in calling it, to the amusement of the Gypsies—but we noticed that his fully armed men were positioned everywhere among the trees.

A few days later the game warden, who had acted as the go-between, came to give le Chef the full account. I was surprised to learn how they differentiated between those who hunted and those who did not, rather than between the enemy oppressors and the victims. The well-born Masters of the Hunt, they shared a sense of high ceremony and, despite differences in language, they spoke the peculiar hunters' Latin, that lingo of euphemism in which the animals "sweat" but don't bleed, and which distinguishes prey as high game (*Hochwild,* boar, doe, fox, and hare) fit to be hunted only by the nobility, as against low or small game (*Niederwild*), fit only for the peasantry.

Through the wilderness we had heard their resonant ceremonial cry of *Horrido! Joho!,* their hails and cheers congratulating successful shots, the marks, and as reply the *Weidmannsdank,* or hunters' thanks, until they were sated, their bags gorged with the kill. Then the bugler blew *Halali,* the final halloo of the day, and we heard in the distance the sound of departing voices. Barring miscalculations, the alarm had been momentary; afterward the forest reverted to its melancholy silence. Contact had been avoided. A polite and convenient balance had been maintained. If the local Resistance, represented by the Gentleman of the Manor, would restrain its more extreme elements (and for the moment they were quite content to remain passive, seeing as how the Resistance was an auxiliary paramilitary unit to be trained, outfitted, held in reserve, and activated only in conjunction with an Allied invasion from abroad), the alien Masters would do likewise—at least for a time. But for the Rom the hunters were already closing in on their quarry. Gypsies were not gentlemen. It was with a growing consternation that the Rom learned how many people still believed in the quaint make-believe prewar normalcy, in the bizarre and tragic masquerade of "rules of war" and the by now clearly equivocal legalism of the Geneva Convention. Unlike le Chef and his easy-going interchangeable companions, the Rom had been exposed to constant inhuman harassment. They had been chased off estates by the landowners' dogs. They could have said to le Chef, "If this can happen to us, it can happen to you." They could have told him the price of optimism. They were born survivors and knew better than I that these were barriers of race, class, and education. Pulika had said, probably facetiously, that in our lives atrocities did not happen every day.

A few days later we had our first Sunday in camp. Like almost no other people on earth, the Rom observed no recurring day of rest or sabbath. Routine or regularity of any kind was foreign to them. Life was a succession of cycles of unpredictable duration and intensity, joyfully punctuated only by the celebration of occasional encounters with their own kin, when for a more or less limited duration they enjoyed one another's company. These celebrations of friendship they called *patshiva* and they were often worthy of legend. They sporadically eased the hardships of everyday Romany life.

We were made aware that it was Sunday by numerous small indications. Everyone at the camp slept one hour longer than usual; then, when they assembled for the daily roll call, no tasks were allotted aside from guard or lookout duties. Breakfast was not served. The men gathered in small groups and it became obvious to us that they were waiting for something to happen. One of le Chef's adjutants even looked at his watch, implying coordination of activities with the "outside." All activities within camp life were on our own self-imposed discipline, rhythm, and use of the day. Far off one of the lookouts perched high in the trees signaled and the leisurely expectant mood became more subdued and a touch more solemn. The man for whom they waited was the Roman Catholic chaplain of the underground army. One of the *marcassins* had gone out to fetch him and he carried a leather bag containing the crucifix, the liturgical vestments, the chalice, prayerbook, and other prerequisites for sacramental dispensation.

Mass was said in a small clearing where a rustic tablelike altar had been built from stakes of birchwood. The men stood bareheaded, self-consciously stiff and awkward. A few of the Rom had been invited to attend. They were hushed and seemed distinctly out of place. It was difficult for them to dissociate the religious ritual from the funerary rites, the only Catholic services to which any of the Rom had been exposed. The fact that for the Gaje it was a weekly occurrence only filled them with wonder, though they were impressed by the extent to which the Gaje could believe what to the Rom was unbelievable: an anthropomorphic god who was a just and omnipotent father to his children, but who was prejudiced against all others, including Gypsies.

The forest stood high and powerful about us. "Monsieur" l'Aumonier said mass. Some of the men stood in apparent devotion, others abstracted or inattentive. As they kneeled or crossed themselves, the Rom followed their example. Candles flickered on the altar, their flames paled to transparency by the slanting rays of the sun. In a daydreamlike reflection I saw in my mind the bodies of the massacred. The silver birch stakes of the improvised altar evoked hollow weathered bones. Barely discernible, the flame on the altar died out, and though I must have tried I could not forget the putrefaction and disintegration to which all flesh was susceptible, the dispersion once robbed of its individual life. "Amen," said the priest, drawing me out of my reverie. In a single file the men went forward and knelt to receive communion. The intermittent high trilling sounds of a bird rose in counterpoint. After a last benediction the service was over.

Shortly afterward, breakfast was served. Until lunch most of the men played *belote* instead of taking apart, cleaning, greasing, and reassembling their weaponry as they did the other six days of the week. After lunch they all assembled again at a bigger clearing in another part of the forest for another Sunday ritual—the soccer game. For the occasion the urban contingent changed into shorts. Le Chef and his staff were divided equally between opposing sides. The game was played with vigor. Some of the local men who had seemed dour and clannish played like lighthearted boisterous boys. In the heart of each action, "Monsieur" l'Aumonier jumped about, ran, gauged, and yelled. He was the referee and played out his chosen role with a passion that belied the first impression of him, that of a devout and austere priest. The scene had all the exuberance and occasional overimpulsiveness of recreation time in a boys' school.

Monsieur Henri, in exchange for services, had offered the Rom temporary shelters for the women and children, for the old and the sick. They had accepted his concern, but without thanks. The Rom were wary of any constricting commitment to the Gaje, even when, as in this case, it spelled safety for them. "He who feeds the pig also holds the knife over it when it is fattened" (*Kon khakhavel o balo wi leste si i shuri*).

Many of the Rom of our *kumpania* spent a few weeks— some even a few months—at remote partisan forest or mountain hideouts. After delivering some explosives, Yojo, Kore, and I visited one nearby Gypsy settlement. The women and children rushed at us screaming and yelling and had to be sharply told to be quiet lest they attract attention. Though we were deep in the woods, some precautions had to be observed, even if only for discipline's sake, the maquis responsible acidly remarked. We sensed tension. The Gypsies, starved of contact with their own kind, were insatiable and rattled away excitedly, asking questions about the outside world, by which they meant the outside world of the Rom at large. They said to us, "We are not moles. Then why should we live like them?" We were suddenly made aware of the gloom of these woods; the smell of fermentation and of damp clothes forced-dried by the fire was everywhere. "If we stay much longer, we will all be white as cheese, like the others," they complained, "and we will smell like them too."

The camp was called, with romantic woodsman's lore, "The Badgers," but the Gypsies persisted in calling it derogatorily

"The Moles," *l Vakandoka*. The children cried that they were hungry, and the women begged to be allowed out, "to provide at least some chicken for dinner. . . ." The man in charge of the adjoining maqui camp, whose nickname was Negus, pointed out that the wood abounded with wildlife. His men laid snares, built and baited traps. "What is the matter with these Gypsies. Are they too spoiled to live off the woods as we do, to take what nature provides?" he asked. The old prejudices came up and he could not refrain from adding, ". . . instead of always stealing our chickens." He was obviously speaking as a farmer and about the past.

The Rom had strict dietary laws regulating what they could and what they could not eat. Horsemeat was *marhime,* forbidden as ritually impure, and for daring to eat it a man could be banished from the tribe and from the community of the Rom in general. Almost as abominable was the eating of game and all animals that were wild and free, like the Rom themselves.

It was obvious that some of the friction was due to the wearing tension of passively waiting and from the fact that the men of the nearby Resistance units were men without women, whereas the Gypsy contingent consisted primarily of women without men. In those days peace seemed remote and, initially as a joke, they had wondered aloud what would happen to them if the war were to last one hundred years. The joke had grown into a miserable obsession.

At first the children had had free access to the opposite camp where their presence had brought more distraction than annoyance. Some children had started to learn the alphabet, but at all times the women had remained diffident and intractable. They had been asked to take in washing and to do mending for the Gaje men, but they had highhandedly rejected this suggestion too. To their hosts this had seemed unusually unreasonable and unaccommodating, while for the Gypsy women even the thought of having to touch other men's clothes was inconceivably repulsive. Yet under circumstances of prolonged and forced proximity, a gradual deterioration of the quality of Gypsy life could not be avoided. The women became indolent and irritable. Often they elected to leave their safe havens, impulsively returning to the open country, increasing their visibility and hastening the fatal confrontation with the Germans. Why suffer now for what might lay beyond? Little in the past had proved worth waiting for.

I knew that the Rom were capable of incredible bursts of energy but not of long or sustained efforts, but had never had occasion to verify under stress their fluid nature and ineradicably nomadic temperament; nor had I, in my wishful thinking, realized how fundamentally they differed from sedentary cultures. To my despair, they proved impervious to reason. In spite of their legendary cunning and their wily insight into the psychology of others (as shown in their fortune-telling abilities), most of the Rom could not bring themselves to admit the insane liability of their obstinate refusal to stay in hiding. There was a Romani saying: "The eyes can see everything except themselves."

At other times and in different regions we went to see the Rom in hiding to check on their situation. We had been given as local "contact" a man who ran a general store. We only knew him as *Furret*, weasel. We did not know if this was his surname, nickname, or code name. I remember, before having met him, wondering if I should address him as Mr. Weasel. He was a fat, jolly, red-faced man and neither his appearance nor personality matched the name he had been given. "Ah," he exclaimed, within hearing of all his customers, "you must have come to visit our Gypsy guests! Sure, sure, take the local trolley omnibus train at 4:15. I will meet you there to introduce you around."

It seemed to us that half the local inhabitants knew whom we came to see, and by inference, who we were; but we had no choice. We took the rickety little train, embarrassed only by the Weasel's exaggerated but well-intentioned concern. The tracks cut a narrow channel through the dense underbrush. In some parts of the woods it disappeared in a tunnel of vegetation. The tracks were invaded by abundant wildflowers. The deep-throated whistle chattered frequently until we stopped for no apparent reason. There was no station or signal. The rails ahead of us and those behind reflected the late afternoon sun. They swept in a wide arc at the base of a mountain. The silence of the forest replaced the chug-chugging. A large number of small sturdily built wooden crates were unhurriedly hauled off. To judge from the efforts of the men handling them, they appeared unusually heavy for their apparent volume. They contained ammunition. They were stacked haphazardly alongside the tracks without any effort being made at concealing them. As we remained on board, the train engineer told us, almost as an afterthought, "You stay here with the crates. They will be around to collect them before nightfall."

At the camp we found a large group of Gypsies and they seemed happy there. The men of the underground army occasionally slipped away in the night to go to the surrounding villages to make love to their women. We spent several days there, as in a dream we feared would end too soon, trying to forget the madness of war.

The camp was surrounded by low overhanging shrubs and dense underbrush providing a welcome sense of privacy and seclusion. It was located near the shores of a lake. The gently rippling water was brownish green and abounded with fish. The reflections of the sun on the water created a strobe light effect. The aromatic shrubs and grass near the edge of the lake were a more tender green and the cool breeze wafted the smell of water. Fat light-brown bumblebees hovered over it.

From a distance I watched Gypsy women washing clothes. They crouched or stood on a cluster of heroic-sized boulders jutting out of the water, their rounded shapes strangely sensuous, their surface unusually smooth. The dark gray color was marked by wet footsteps of bare feet. The women wore deep, wild, exotic colors, jarringly out of tune with the placid pastoral tranquillity of the surroundings.

We who had come from the outside world were subject to a permanent anxiety based not on delusion, but on reality; we could only marvel at the existence of this oasis of disquieting unconcern.

CHAPTER EIGHT

When we left the *marcassins'* camp, several Gypsy families remained behind with Yojo as intermediary with le Chef and his "guests." Pulika promised to return, circumstances permitting, at widely spaced intervals and with great precautions. Le Chef assumed the provisioning of his guests in exchange for "services rendered." Both "Monsieur" l'Aumonier and le Chef had asked Pulika, and therefore the other men of our *kumpania,* to establish contact on their behalf with units in other regions and to assist in the transportation of arms. The particular instruction appeared to me at first a trifle vague but did not seem to bother the other Rom. It occurred to me that sheltering a large number of our family group might also represent to le Chef hostages of a sort, a bargaining point for both parties.

We traveled in several light four-wheeled canvas-covered vans. The horses were in poor condition and they incessantly skidded on the pine-needled ground. We were forced to make frequent detours because the forest growth was too dense and the closeness of the trees allowed not enough space for the wagons. Along our way branches would whip and bend. Dead tree limbs crashed down or were caught in the younger trees. We dared not stop to cook food or prepare coffee or even smoke for fear of lighting the dry tinder, even though it had recently rained. We emerged from the already darkened forest and stopped for the night at the edge of some flooded marshy flatlands, but we were too late. It was already too dark to make a fire. We bedded down to sleep away our hunger. The night was cool and heavy with mist. The days were growing shorter and at the edge of the forest leaves were falling. Through the gathering night came the smell from a nearby but unseen thicket of aromatic bushes blending with the cool muddy smell of marshes. I suddenly realized this was a welcome relief from the overwhelming perfume of the deep forest.

I awakened in predawn darkness and saw our small wagon camp invaded by strands and patches of moonlit fog, and I heard the soft babbling of flowing water. A purifying wind was blowing. I let myself imagine the damp and velvety smooth touch of the fog moving about undissolved memories of those wantonly destroyed. By daybreak the moonlit fog had changed into plain early morning mists. After the rain the high seedy grasses were full of snails. Everything felt clammy. The soggy kindling gave off abundant white smoke and just enough heat to boil the water for coffee. The only water we could draw was as opaque as milk. We harnessed the horses and hitched them to the vans. For a short way their hooves splashed through puddles before we turned onto the winding highway from the rugged wooded hills. Birds sat in sullen clusters on the untilled fields or between rows of stunted corn. We met some German military trucks, but no one paid any attention to us. For a time we traveled from hamlet to hamlet in what might have appeared an erratic course. The men traded whatever and wherever they could; the women told fortunes in exchange for farm produce in preference to money. One evening at dusk an old woman approached one of the Gypsy women to have her fortune told and said that her husband, the local gravedigger, would like to talk to the Gypsies but was too shy to do so. Would the Gypsies be willing to meet him at a certain spot under any kind of pretext? The Rom suggested buying a gold watch. Contact had been made.

The following night Zurka and I were picked up by an old farmer driving a buggy. We shook hands with him silently and together went into a night of new adventure. On the open road several men on bicycles joined us, some slightly ahead, others close behind. At last information, he said abruptly, there were no German special units in the immediate neighborhood. Curfew was a fiction, and, wishing us well, he sank back into silence. We stopped at a large farmhouse squatting in the fields, outlined against the sky, and we heard the reassuring rumbling sounds of cattle lowing inside the stables. Bypassing the sprawling buildings and the haylofts, we crawled through a barbed-wire fence and into the pasture lands. Several of the bicycle riders joined us, while others spread out over a wide area. At close range we realized most of them were very young. Closely followed by a very young boy, the taciturn old peasant who had brought us was inspecting the hedges. They looked at them with a strangely professional thoroughness which impressed us very much, especially since we had no idea what the proceedings would lead to. An appreciative low whistle brought us to the spot, even though we were reluctant to show our ignorance and puzzlement at what they were doing. A large wild rabbit had gotten itself caught and had strangled trying to disentangle itself. The old farmer was simply a poacher collecting from his snares. We had to admit that it did provide him with plausible cover.

We waited in the chill night, watching and listening. A light wind was blowing and the men wondered if the plane would come. Then, barely audible above the singing of the wind, we heard a far-off throbbing sound. For a while we could not clearly make out if it was the sound of approaching trucks—which could only mean the Germans—or if it were the British military supply plane we expected. The dry barking of German antiaircraft guns far to the northwest gave us a clue. In a sudden burst of activity men were piling firewood at three different spots. They waited anxiously for a signal to light them. The throbbing died away and again we waited, wide awake now, more tense than before. After a few minutes the sound was back, unmistakably from the air though from a slightly different direction than before. The first time must have been an evasive maneuver. The sound rapidly grew louder and then it seemed almost overhead. The fires were lit and from one corner of the field a blinker light flashed signals rapidly. The plane passed, veered, and came back directly overhead; a huge crushing shadow emphasized the deafening roar of the motors. The fires were already being frantically scattered and extinguished.

The plane flew incredibly low. We could feel the plane's air-wash; it had been like standing in the path of an onrushing locomotive.

Wherever they were, the Germans must have been alerted. We had to leave the location with the utmost speed and circumspection. The seconds it took for the containers to land seemed interminable. Everything happened simultaneously. We watched the long metal cylinders come hurling down from the plane's belly. After a short fall the parachutes opened with a snapping sound. Gone was the powerful black lumbering presence of the low-flying bomber. The throbbing died away and for a while there was complete silence. The containers, suspended from their parachutes, swayed gently in the moon-light. They landed with a crunch about two hundred feet from the signal fires. It had been an exceptionally good drop. The men ran to collect the packages. They frantically folded and bundled the huge unwieldy parachutes to erase the damning evidence. Everything was transported and hidden and after-ward the men dispersed, taking with them the rabbits and the copper-wire snares.

Two teenage boys took us back by bicycle, we sitting sideways on the frame. They pedaled leisurely, swaying from side to side on the path. A thin stretched rabbit hung from the steering handle by its hindlegs, a molting shaggy mess of matted fur of rust color running into light gray below, the plumed tail fringed in white. The long limp ears, ragged at the edge, trailed the ground. The wide-open eyes were staring and frightened even in death. In the hours waiting for the plane it had been gutted and its entrails removed except for its heart and liver. Shortly it would be stewed with prunes. In the meantime it brushed irritatingly against my leg in an off beat with the pedaling. There was a gentle cool air current and the night was very quiet; the open skies were full of stars. The landscape was of desolate fields in the moonlight and of pastures fenced in by three barbed wires stretched between stakes. There were few trees and those there were were naked and leafless.

The teenage boys, with whom we had not exchanged any conversation at all, stopped at a crossroad between fields, dropped us off, and departed silently. We mumbled goodnight, to which, we thought, they grunted back as they pedaled away. They carried out instruction—nothing less, nothing more. The old peasant with the limp had driven away in the opposite direction. The containers were piled in his carriage and covered with a tarpaulin. Bicycle riders preceded him, others followed in silent rear guard.

Looking around for a moment, we found we were near our wagon camp and realized that the old peasant was the only one to know where we belonged. The boys had been told to leave us at a certain crossroad believing that there we would be picked up by still a different escort.

The old gravedigger's wife came again. The following day before daybreak a long file of peasant vans (pulled by old nags and driven by Gypsies) with superstructures covered with patched tarpaulins in subtle shades of sun- and rain-bleached grays and browns and blacks hobbled along a little-used dirt road past the spreading graveyard. As a rule Gypsies shunned cemeteries, yet now they halted alongside its low stone wall. Like a ghost, the taciturn old peasant with the lame foot suddenly materialized. At a signal from him several older men came out of hiding from among the sheltering graves. Pointing toward several newly filled-in graves, the topsoil of which still clearly showed recent spadework, he said with a touch of macabre malice that he wished there were many more like that. The old men in the meantime were loading onto the wagons crates of ammunition and arms which they had held for us in safekeeping. The old gravedigger had effec-tively combined and solved the problems of transportation and safe storage. The Rom did not, at least at that time, noticeably appreciate the specifics nor his sense of humor. As we left the area, it might have occurred to a shrewd and suspicious ob-server that the wagons pulled heavily and rode a trifle too low on their haunches. But since they were Gypsy wagons nobody paid them much heed.

On another occasion we were invited to receive "friends." We had to wait out several nights only to leave at dawn, cold and frustrated. The confirmation message, a cryptic quotation making sense only to those concerned, had been received over the regular BBC broadcasts. Possibly the weather over England had been unfavorable. We waited warmly bundled up in our sheepskin coats with scarfs wrapped around our throats. It was more humid than truly cold. The dropping zone (D.Z. in technical parlance) was as usual prepared and manned by an alert and experienced "reception committee." Once or twice we had had false alerts—dogs barking unaccountably in the night at some isolated farmhouse; a German truck convoy rumbling by over the main road south; antiaircraft guns ack-acking far away; and then nothing more. Then unexpectedly the plane was there almost before we had enough time to light the straw fires. A light wind had extenuated and deflected the sound of the airplane motors and it had suddenly materialized at a much higher altitude than we had anticipated. The men ran to take position.

This time we were to receive "friends" rather than "packages." We anxiously watched the plane's underside perhaps a thousand feet above us. Maybe they wouldn't drop. Maybe they had failed to see our signals at the time of fly-by. Then a small dark shape fell tumbling out. As the parachute flapped open it jolted and hesitated in what seemed from the ground like a swaying stand-still. The plane rushed on. Farther along another dark shape fell out. We watched aghast at what we evaluated, making allowance for wind drift, could be a mile or possibly more of error. Two men went off at a dogtrot to meet him upon impact. We looked back at number one coming down rapidly now. The wind was flapping his parachute like a breeze playing with a flag. More objects—people—popped out of the airplane's belly miles farther on. Instinctively looking back to check on the various ejected shapes, we saw one of them plunging down to earth at giddying speed, gyrating all the while. It squirmed and danced. It fell faster and faster, spiraling. The shape, by now distinctly human, went limp. It hit the ground. The wind-swollen parachute, apparently damaged and out of control, looked like a misshapen unnatural moon. The smooth silky conveyance buckled, tension slackened (apparently it had been punctured), and deflated in a slow-motion collapse. His parachute had snarled and he fell to his death.

We watched another parachute and found in its eerily placid descent a sense of escape from immediate reality. The giant mushroom lazily hit the ground. Manipulating the lines, the man suspended from it fell sideways. For a moment he lay still. Almost simultaneously several men converged on the spot. They helped him disentangle himself and get up while the others quickly rolled up his chute. He was dazed and we knew that he had seen his partner crash. The men awkwardly patted him on the shoulders and back to convey their sympathy. He stood slightly swaying, his legs spread wide for balance. With an impersonal disdain in his unseeing eyes, he gazed at them without blinking. Facing him, the peasant boys were awed and uncertain, carefully guarding their inner feelings. They were still and deliberate, angular and emphatic in their movements, and tentative at making contact.

The wind was blowing stronger and from the northwest. In a voice only slightly lower than normal, but impressively even and controlled, he casually related to us how his friend had said in challenge as he sat with his legs over the edge of the plane's jump hole, "See you down there. I'll race you to it!" We felt ill at ease about his chilling show of callousness, or toughness, or whatever it was that could make him detached from the death of his companion. Strangely, we envied him for this iron-nerved self-control. He completed his thought by adding: "And he won."

Then he jack-knifed in a sudden forward movement, hiding his face in both hands, weeping. This awakened to reality the men who made haste to hustle him away. Daybreak was near and we were running out of time. The most we had was mastery of the night and could not allow daylight to reveal us in the open. In the distance, still shaded by dusk, we could see our restless men on the alert for danger signals. As I looked in the direction where the dead man lay I saw the men there moving about briskly. I remembered our friend the gravedigger and instinctively wished he were there. The men removed a clumsy-looking package which I knew to be the

undoubtedly horribly mangled corpse wrapped in his parachute as shroud. This time it was without envy that I admired
and was grateful for those men who "knew how to do things"
and who were not squeamish. The "unlikely worst" had happened.

Monsieur Henri had implied that at an early stage specialists would feel wasted. The repeated drops over widely
scattered areas in turn implied that the time was coming when
specialists would *not* feel wasted.

On another night we allowed ourselves to be taken to a
remote backcountry location, despite deep misgivings which
Kore and I had talked about and agreed were fantasies rather
than premonitions. For reasons I have forgotten we were to
witness an important drop because a particular segment of the
movement wanted to show that it was "receiving."

The field was a windswept emptiness. We stood among trees
stripped by autumn winds, leaning against their trunks. The
nighttime vigil was long and the men stood waiting in a restless and somewhat aggressive mood. We were outsiders representing "them"—those whom I knew in an equally unsatisfac-
tory manner as the "coordinating authority." I realized they
resented our show of authority. They were as arrogant as we
were patronizing and in turn they tried to impress us by projecting an image of sullen ruthlessness. In contrast to us, they
were heavily armed and looked like the kind who would fancy
themselves safer that way.

The intermittent barking of distant dogs put us on edge but
the men were on home ground and paid scant attention. As
we heard the plane approach the regulation signal fires were
quickly lit in triangular formation to signify our specific location for pin-point dropping. I had a sudden renewed apprehension when I thought I heard a steady humming sound
rather than the more uneven throbbing of our own planes, but
the plane was overhead almost at treetop level. The roar was
deafening, but though the plane loomed unusually low it
seemed smaller than expected. There followed an unanticipated
burst of very rapid machine-gun fire from what we then knew

to be a German fighter. A stream of bullets dug up the ground in a diagonal line from where we stood. There was an acrid smell of cordite. An enemy plane disguised as British performed incredible aerial acrobatics to turn and strafe us again. Each maneuver forced him higher and more to the left of us. The location fires were wildly scattered to the winds, but the glowing embers could not be thoroughly stamped out and gave us away. One of the men standing next to us, so hard and arrogant a second before, lay motionless, horribly injured. Like a kill-mad shark, the plane turned upward and came back again soaring higher still. A flare explored harshly lighting up a scene of panicky disarray and massacre.

We ran madly across the unknown country. Trucks grinding furiously drove up the main road and then shooting erupted far to our right. Dogs were barking. The Germans had really prepared a feast. For a moment longer the flat countryside was alive with men running. Many more than I had realized were involved in our "operation." In total disarray and in breach of solidarity we were left by the others to our own devices and we ran aimlessly. We ran until our lungs felt as if about to burst; gasping for air, the pressure of breathing painfully racked our throats, our brains were icily clear but inoperative—somehow short-circuited. Now and then guns chattered in the night. Then the isolated monotonous staccato bursts of submachine guns, irritating as the dripping of a faulty faucet, tapered off before dawn.

I remained trembling, isolated in the immediacy of hurt, fear, and exhaustion beyond my worst expectations, raging at the knowledge of my physical limitations. After some deep reviving draughts of air, I became vaguely aware that Kore too had stopped running and must be recovering somewhere nearby. We had to recuperate our strength. We had to move on. There was no safety in just lying there hidden by the night. It would have been easier to be destroyed while in flight. I had wondered while running not *if* I would be hit by a bullet, but rather *where* it would find me, what sensation it would cause, and if death would be long or short in coming.

The serenity that followed with resting up seemed even

more frightening because I knew we had to outwit the vigilance of the Germans. For that matter we also had to beware of the anger and treachery of the local peasants. Understandably they resented and feared the violence we had unwittingly loosed. By apprehending and surrendering us to the Germans, they could hope to lessen reprisals against themselves and their village. Unknown to them, the inhabitants of the nearest village had been endangered by our clandestine use of this locality for "dropping." They had reason for grievance against us. In our wake, and in that of others actively fighting the common enemy, whole villages were given over to silence and the spreading weeds. In this too our dilemma was stamped with tragic irony: we became instrumental in destroying those whom we meant to benefit and protect. After a wait of indeterminate length, Kore crept to where I was. We kept close together. About us were gently rolling hills dotted with cultivated areas now bare and plowed over, totally devoid of possible cover. As the day rose and light broke through the night we walked rapidly, trusting only our luck. This time luck was a country cemetery with a strangely abundant growth of wild grasses and tall weeds. We lay down in a narrow hollow alongside, or rather half underneath, the projecting ridge of a funeral monument. In the distance cocks crowed, dogs barked, trucks rattled, pigs squealed and grunted, horses neighed, and occasionally a man cracked his whip. Overhead in narrow flight formation Luftwaffe planes flew back with the dawn from bombing English cities. Within the boundaries of the cemetery we found a sense of protection and overcome by its immediate stillness we slept dreamlessly. As Pulika said, only life made sense. No use ruminating any longer about the undone, the refused, the ungiven. Lying in the shadow of an unknown grave I learned how much I wanted life.

When twilight was about to fall the distant noises of the world outside our secluded sanctuary came to their ends. We left our narrow confine and walked about to warm up and shake off the stiffness of our prolonged physical inactivity and the penetrating cold of the graveyard. We were thirsty, hungry, and weak. Under the cover of a gentle evening rain we slipped out of the cemetery, careful not to trample the weeds so as to leave as little trace as possible of our passage. We wandered in the meadows through the night silence looking for dandelions or other edibles. The hard green leaves were bitter and tough and only sharpened our hunger by activating our digestive juices. Briefly we considered stealing some fowls, but making a fire to roast them on was out of the question, besides the noise the chickens would make if we attempted to catch them inside the crowded chicken coop. In the daytime we could not move abroad when it would be easy enough to catch them scratching the earth, more obsessed with feeding themselves than with their security. In a meadow we found some well-fed cows with milk-swollen udders. They looked at us placidly with their veiled eyes. Kore expertly pulled the pink teats and a violent narrow jet of milk squirted in his dark felt hat. We drank from the clumsy makeshift container. The milk spilled over the border and darkened the felt as it slowly seeped through. We drank greedily and unconcerned. The milk was frothy, lukewarm, bland, and strong smelling. We each drank overly large quantities in impatient gulps which left us breathless and which lay uncomfortably heavy in our stomachs. The pangs of hunger were stilled but the meal left us nauseated. We returned to our shelter and decided to let a few more days pass before attempting to leave, hoping that by then the enemy's vigilance would have slackened. We stayed up all night, moving constantly to keep somewhat warm in our damp clothes. Our anger, fear, and frustration lacked duration and we ceased to care beyond the immediate: to get through the night, and then through the following day, and, if we still had the endurance and the good sense, through the next night and the day that followed thereafter. We would not allow exposure and hunger to drain the will out of us. We would float like corks. Shivering with fever we withdrew into self-willed short-term hibernation.

In midafternoon the next day we were startled by the sound of a woman weeping. Neither one of us had heard her coming. She knelt praying beside a grave startlingly near us. The sweet smell of the garden flowers she had brought came to haunt us with inappropriately morbid thoughts of funerals and death. We had to be even more silent and immobile lest we startle her. Perversely our young bodies and nerves wanted to move, to squirm, to cough, to sneeze, to jump up and run.

After she left we avidly drank the water from the metal container in which her flowers stood. She must have brought that water a long way from home. The milk had appeased our hunger but left our thirst unslaked. The water already tasted of the juice of cut plants but we were grateful for it.

Then one day we awakened in a world white with hoarfrost and we knew we had to move that night lest we freeze to death. After indulging for a last time in the plentiful milk supply, we walked through the night. Before daybreak caught us in the open we found an adequate hiding place. Warmed as we were by the long march and exhilarated by the action, we slept soundly, to awaken violently at the sound of machine guns. We instinctively located their direction. Distraught, angry, and sweating, yet controlling the instinct to run, we lay low. After a few seconds we wondered at the uncommonly long burst of gunfire. The Germans were trained to shoot in short bursts. Also the cadence seemed slower than that of the customary German MG-34s. It continued at an even pace seemingly forever, slowly moving away from us. The sound puzzled us more than it disturbed us. It was too long, too slow, and moving away from us. Against our better judgment we crawled to a better vantage point only to discover a bent old peasant pushing an empty wheelbarrow rattling loudly over the cobblestone pavement. The unexpected denouement broke for us the tension and anxiety of the recent past, no doubt intensified by hunger, cold, and lack of sleep. It was like a return from delirium giving us in the process a surprising feeling of purely physical well-being. We left our hiding place and with a show of recklessness walked self-assured and boldly in the open and in broad daylight. The terrain was still unfamiliar, possibly even threatening, but we no longer cared about it.

We passed some old men sitting on a low wooden bench smoking their pipes in the early morning sun. We simultaneously greeted one another even though strangers. We had passed. We no longer were hunted beasts. Our inner emotional condition was not, as we had assumed, like a jaundice visible to all. We entered the combined local tavern and general store where we ordered coffee and brandy and were reintegrated into the routine of everyday life. We had money. Instead of being worthless and obsolete, as when we were outlaws, we were again a functioning beneficent commodity.

Kore asked to be allowed to make an urgent telephone call. There was no telephone in this village, only in the next. Reassured, we sat back to enjoy the walls and smoke-blackened ceiling in contrast to the immensity of open space. We enjoyed the comfort-giving warmth of the coffee, the euphoria of the alcohol. It was like coming home after a long and dangerous illness with a renewed sense of gratitude for what others with the unconscious egoism of health took for granted. After a long and tormenting waiting period, so as not to awaken the suspicion of the peasants (in whom the distrust of strangers was inbred), we broke our fast with a meal of boiled potatoes, black bread, smoked ham, and hard-boiled eggs. We bought tobacco and with a feeling of shameless indulgence rolled ourselves cigarette after cigarette. Our feeling of unextinguishable well-being and reckless self-assurance was not dampened even when the first German we met gave us a long unpleasant stare.

CHAPTER NINE

We went back to Paris to seek ever deepening commitment, to urge Monsieur Henri to let us participate in new opportunities, to demand the right to fight. Too many of our activities now appeared to us peripheral.

After a final briefing and a ritual parting word of confidence, we went out into the waiting night fully armed. We had come into the area separately, by public conveyance, but over a staggered period of several days and even then we had waited out our time. Besides Kore, there were Laetshi and myself. We knew some of the other men but had never before worked with them. We were apprentices under the supervision of a specialist and were expected to provide armed cover—what they called "safety enforcement procedure."

To all appearances the specialist was an unassuming man with a deceptively ordinary face, but we knew his mission to be rather out of the ordinary. Some would perhaps have detected a certain undefinable hardness in his eyes. During the earlier briefing he had shown a ruthless unerring simplicity. He was the kind of man who unconsciously inspired men to outdo themselves for him.

As we approached the target area I recognized the location from the briefing, even in semidarkness. It had the surreal familiarity experienced only in dreams. We moved about cautiously but unafraid and spread out among the sparse trees, mating our shapes to theirs to lessen the visibility of our number. The nameless, faceless specialist (for in a way all strangers are masked) detached himself from the rest of the group in his function of "demolition expert." His two assis-

128

tants collected from us the compact lethal packages we had carried along with dread and pride. They moved carefully and unemotionally. We kept watch while our sweat-soaked clothes unpleasantly chilled us in the serene night. From a distance we followed the operation with awe. They handled the explosives with quick skillful movements yet with the circumspection and precision of a clinical operation. The pounding of our hearts made it difficult to listen to sounds from outside which might indicate danger abroad. As far as the darkness allowed, I followed their figures moving quickly along the railroad tracks until the night swallowed them up. We waited for their return to "evacuate the area," but not before watching the action from a good vantage point a short distance away. We huddled crouched for what seemed like most of the night. We were told not to speak or smoke and the wait became unnervingly anticlimactic. A soft hissing sound produced between clenched teeth sharply drew me out of incoherent reverie and back to the present insane reality of our situation. A faint distant rumble quickly materialized in the emberlike glow and thunder of a locomotive approaching with the irresistible thrust of an onrushing assault tank. Elated and petrified, we stared breathless with anticipation, fearing that something, anything, had gone wrong. In seemingly jumbled order and deranged sequence the titanic locomotive blew up in a burst of sparks, swerved right, and jolted to a halt. Sucking in a deep breath I experienced an interval of incredible silence like the sudden stopping of a rain shower. The noise ceased so abruptly that I felt as if I would have a sudden lack of air.

I was seized by a sense of fierce exaltation, a frighteningly unsuspected rapture of destruction, a drunkenness strangely more satisfying than that of wine. We too now possessed the power to terrify and destroy. I experienced a sense of weightlessness. Dumb with horror, I felt the stupendous blast as the burst of sparks, smoke, and flaming debris rose into the sky. The locomotive tender was smashed and the wagons were ripped up, buckled, folded, or caved in. Then followed several additional delayed blasts. Clouds of dense dirty gray steam shot out screaming from the mangled boiler. The disconnected locomotive kept moving frantically like a great animal clawing at the specter of death. Steam was escaping through its dislocated whistle. Then there followed a final blast.

Kore gave me an insinuating look. Between Kore and myself had grown an awareness beyond that to which brothers are born. We dispersed silently in different directions.

Weirdly lit by the fire raging below, a tall column of smoke rose high into the sky. German soldiers jumped clear of the wrecked wagons and threw themselves on the ground for cover, arms at the ready as if they expected an attack. Others, officers probably, swarmed along inspecting the mangled tortured steel of the ripped-up railroad tracks. The bedlam was strangely underlined by the plaintive hooting of a locomotive shunting in the distance. The demolition expert had vanished in the night. We never saw him again.

There followed many such actions. During the following months Kore, myself, and several other of the Lowara and also Tshurara youths served our gradual apprenticeship under lesser masters. Some raids were abortive, others shatteringly effective. There were others from which some operatives did not return.

Actions were masterminded by "the command" and we were told when and where to strike. The German-controlled press referred to our operations simply as acts of banditry and tried to underplay their effectiveness. But by reporting them occasionally, possibly as a warning, they were admitting to omens of change, defying the myth of their absolute supremacy. It demonstrated the ability to penetrate supposedly secure and well-protected military areas. It forced the occupiers to spread themselves out too thin and over too many potential crisis areas to be effective. It forced them to keep on special alert duties additional powerline, railroad, and other specialized repairmen. It wore down their morale while they were fighting on other fronts. We did not fail to admit that the Germans had the means to put an end to our activities and eliminate the nuisance value we represented; we knew they could do so only if we were a matter of priority. We were informed and advised when to strike and when to hide, even when to evacuate an area completely, in case special pressure was about to be exerted by their repression agencies. In the meantime, we worked like termites.

Kore, Zurka, Laetshi, and I were scouting for special talent, recruiting, and also partly involved in training. Kore revealed himself an excellent teacher. More and more youths of both the Lowara and the Tshurara tribes became involved and our specialties were further diversified. The "high actions" grew to be a tacit reward for meeting performance pledges in less sought after jobs. We formed a fairly small organization with far-flung operations practically all over the German-occupied territories with the exception of the invaded part of the U.S.S.R.

The Gypsies' participation in one particular area of special services began trivially, if not foolishly. When Pulika and other men from our *kumpania* had, after some initial hesitation, registered in order to obtain ration cards, they had kept registering in different localities with an extensive number of identity papers of different nationalities. These, obviously, had been of doubtful authenticity, yet had gone undetected. After the initial mutual commitment between the coordinating authorities and the Gypsies, the latter had contributed a substantial amount of ration cards to the movement. As the movement grew, so did its needs. One source always accessible was the independent black market, but for this substantial funds were needed; the other was illegally obtained ration cards. At a certain point it was decided that monthly "lifting" of distribution centers would be in order. A segment of the Rom accepted the responsibility of organizing these raids, but they recruited and relied on professional burglars because, for all their reputation, the Rom were never burglars or housebreakers. After several months of successful large-scale and far-flung raids on distribution centers, they were put under heavy guard. This in turn forced us to armed holdups. There were mishaps but the trend could not be halted.

The short, intense bursts of energetic action suited the Gypsy character well. The women, children, sick, and old remained safe in hiding while the younger men could in this way contribute to their support.

Under the influence either of the opportunistic elements of the "outside experts" or by spontaneous combustion, several men of the Tshurara tribe opted to exert their independence. The catalyst was Bernard, a French safecracker who had come to our attention in connection with a particularly difficult operation which he had handled with superb mastery. Tshurkina and he had unaccountably taken a strong personal liking for one another, and unknown to us had decided to remain in contact.

Bernard was a coarse-faced, unsavory underworld character, past his prime and strongly marked by a debauched life. He was overweight but nimble and spoke with glib facility; with an implicating wink and an insouciant snap of his fingers, he insolently but cleverly mimicked his more persistent critics. He dressed with an underworld flavor especially cherished by *souteneurs* or *mecs,* the pimps. Yet whenever he could he wore carpet slippers typical of the *petit commerçant.* He eagerly kept abreast of the sartorial developments of the Zazous as they became known. They were politically uncommitted youth, vaguely contemptuous of the Germans and of upper-middle-class parents. They affected sophisticated boredom with almost everything except their dress and a budding interest in movie directors. They wore loose overlong jackets and narrow trousers rolled halfway up their shins. They had a predilection for golf shoes and long hair combed into a ducktail in the back. Their feminine campfollowers wore short, narrow, straight skirts and, in contrast to their male counterparts (as in some animal species), pointedly avoided color, ornaments, frills, or flamboyance of any sort. They greeted each other by raising the index finger and wagging it, pronouncing the cryptical *Zazou,* which from password-greeting became their name. Their known spawning grounds were in Paris around the Place Victor Hugo and la Muette. Imitating the Zazou made Bernard feel young and handsome. He was to spend only a short time among the Rom, but his unpleasant way of looking at the Gypsy women with unconcealed greedy glances did not escape his hosts, who, because he was an outsider, chose to ignore it. Unlike the Rom, he had an affinity for violence and displayed more than a streak of barroom brawler or alley fighter. There had been some allegations about a messy killing in which he had been involved, yet he was too useful to be dispensed with. He lived with Tshurkina's family. After successful expeditions he took Tshurkina and his two younger bachelor brothers Vedel and Merikano on ill-advised drinking sprees, introducing them to the clandestine expensive nightlife available in the big cities to war profiteers and blackmarket operators. This was a flagrant contravention to the directives of the *kris* for the Rom not to be conspicuous.

In the beginning the ration card collection operations showed no clear overall pattern. Gradually the authorities, or those working for them, improved their safety precautions and our raids became better organized and more sophisticated. Every month new ration stamps were distributed with a different color and design, kept secret until distribution to prevent possible counterfeiting. They were printed by the central authority of the National Food Distribution Office and were given out by the local distribution centers upon presentation of the holder's permanent ration card backed by his identification papers.

The printing plant of the National Office was impregnable. The raids were therefore directed at various intermediary and subsidiary posts. The time left for collecting the rations was limited to two or three days at the most. Thirty, forty, fifty, and more harvesting raids were made every month in widely scattered parts of the German *Gaue* or military districts. Occasionally an exceedingly efficient or lucky unit managed to lift two or three offices in a well-planned series of raids, like a well-thrown flat stone skipping the water surface. Planning the raids required that an elaborate system of intelligence be gathered, evaluated, and coordinated. Often this came from the horse's mouth, from officials of the National Organization. At first the stamps had simply been kept in a drawer at the town hall or at the home of the official in charge. Guards were posted after a series of embarrassing thefts. Like a raised flag, this gave the raiders confirmation that the goods had arrived and told them where they were to be found. These guards were often the hated *miliciens* or *gendarmes,* which did not restrain the raiders from using excessive "persuasive" force.

Automatic weapons and burglary tools were brought to the scene by assistants with innocuous appearances and once the raid was over the loot was taken away by other assistants, so that the principals in the action came and went free from possible compromising evidence if intercepted by the police. Occasionally the principals responsible for these forays were ardent young Gypsies. More often they were the leading Rom themselves, men of authority still in their early middle age, men who were vigorous and bold and who had decisive bearings, such as Bidshika and his brother Kalia, Punka, Bakro, who gradually displaced the younger unmarried men.

Tshurkina, the son of Pani of the Tshurara tribe, was among the first to join forces with us. He brought with him his fifteen- or sixteen-year-old son Djem, a bright-eyed, stubborn, arrogant boy uncommonly ambitious for a Gypsy. Soon after, they were joined by numerous brothers, cousins, and nephews.

The Lowara tried hard to find safe havens for their families in the forests or in relatively safe distant rural areas. To go on expeditions the men left their families for several days or weeks, most of the time without the possibility of communications. They considered the risks exchange currency for their relatives' safety. For the Rom this kind of life away from their own kind represented a real hardship. They felt the food of the Gaje on which they were forced to subsist to be ill-prepared and lacking in substance and they longed for the usual ways of their people: to be able to squat, eat with their fingers, wipe their fingers on their wives' aprons and to be served by them, to sleep in featherbeds.

One of the first times we had in this fashion slept away from our own we had been in a fairly large group including Zurka, Pitti, Bidshika, Laetshi, and Kore, as well as Bidshika's wife, Tshaya. There had been no Rom camping in the vicinity and so we were forced to accept for the night the lodgings arranged for us. The Rom, none of whom apparently had ever slept in a hotel or in the fashon of the Gaje, were horrified that the beds had sheets. They adamantly refused to sleep between "shrouds." The mattresses were dragged off the bedsteads and put side by side in one single room so that everybody could remain together. Later that night, the Gypsy women knocked at the door shamefacedly begging us to share the room because just the three of them were afraid to sleep isolated from their own surrounded by Gaje.

Long before the war the Tshurara had revealed to us their different ways. They always had been more reckless and rambunctious. They did not mind living constantly on the run. In contravention to the unanimous agreement arrived at by the Rom before the *kris*—to stay out of sight as much as possible and avoid being conspicuous—the Tshurara decided on their own that there was no more need for such exaggerated precautions.

After a tavern brawl several young Tshurara were arrested by the local *gendarmes* who promptly transferred them to the Germans. At an opportune moment, Vedel and his brother Merikano knocked down a guard and overwhelmed him. They ran away and waited out the ensuing commotion and search by hiding under a German military vehicle, hanging from the axles. Later they held up two civilians and, under threats of violence, forced them to undress. Thus disguised they had made their way back to their own. Instead of anticipating the consequences to their people, they trusted in their luck, misreading or willfully disregarding the temper of the time.

After bitter quarrels about these unnecessary risks, we had failed to restrain our more volatile allies. Our earlier suspicions were fully confirmed about the pernicious influence of Bernard in encouraging the Tshurara in their inborn inclination. The Tshurara again started to travel about in their conspicuous ramshackle wagons. Tshurkina's spectacularly beautiful wife Liza once again joined him in wild public drinking at taverns. She was soon joined by her sister Pesha, Shandor's wife, and their brood. As before the war, they indulged in mindless mischief making. The Rom had derived a certain material ease from the commissions they received on their operations and again, in contrast to the Lowara, the majority of the Tshurara enjoyed the extravagant display of their newly achieved affluence. In droves they frequented the flashier dining spots and bars impudently catering to the blackmarket racketeers. The Tshurara men, who wore expensively tailored double-breasted suits, silk shirts, and extravagant light-colored patent-leather shoes, never failed to create a commotion. They were accompanied by the women either barefooted or wearing extra high spike-heeled shoes and followed by their numerous children in cast-off clothing or practically nothing. They willingly paid the exorbitant tariffs and therefore could not be denied. They tipped in royal fashion.

By this time the war had gone on for several years and whatever provisions the people had managed to collect were exhausted. Rationing of food and clothes was stringent and painfully felt everywhere. The blackmarket price of white bread was from twenty to fifty times its legal standard price. People greatly resented this flaunting of plenty.

Persistent rumors had it that for his personal profit Tshurkina was selling excessively large quantities of ration stamps to blackmarket dealers. He and Bernard had repeatedly failed to inform the others about their operations or to render accounts. When asked about this they had pleaded as extenuating circumstances difficulties of communication due to extreme mobility and the imperative need for secrecy. Ignoring rebukes, Tshurkina and his budding gang of non-Gypsy bodyguards and hangers-on continued to scout for safe-crackers and others of the hunter-killer type who found a sense of excitement by living close to death, bringing additional bad elements into their independent organization while the operations ran to unmitigated banditry.

I was in despair; in my youthful egotism I assumed that all this was due to my own errors in judgment. Tshurkina and his associates pursued an ever more defiant course, exciting discord between the Lowara and the Tshurara, eroding the trust among Rom at a time when we needed one another more than ever. The tension exploded into violence and our common commitment for survival lost its cohesion and direction.

I tried to reason with them. I tried to show them the extent of their criminal idiocy in order that they, and we, might escape destruction. But I could not contain either their greed or their restless vitality. The Tshurara moved out into the open, displaying an irrepressible lawlessness and thus became increasingly visible and inviting targets.

Suddenly I was made aware of the futility of my efforts to save the Rom. Among them were people like Tshurkina; there also were some like Pulika. I prayed God that in my own small way I could help prevent the waste of their seed!

If only the Rom, or at least the Lowara, could have made a radical break with Tshurkina and his ilk. But it could not be done. Pulika warned me not to allow the existing tension to develop into an open confrontation with the Tshurara, which I craved with the objectivity of a spurned lover. He wondered at the added absurdity of a war within a war. But we could no longer extricate ourselves; the pull of the stream was too strong.

There followed a rising momentum of raw and ugly violent incidents. After having been forced to admit my misjudgment and moral defeat, I sought a conversation with Monsieur Henri about the matter to explain our dismal retreat from clear commitment. At first Monsieur Henri suggested letting things take their course. Beyond considerations of pure morality (that prewar luxury), I should still appreciate the considerable capacity the Tshurara possessed to damage, to disrupt, and to create grave administrative difficulties for the Germans. Monsieur Henri promised to "put the whole matter under study," but I could not misread his tone: to win the war all means were acceptable. His gaze remained steady, but clouded over, clearly implying his irrevocable disengagement. I withdrew and gradually became disaffected.

There followed a series of actions in which the Tshurara, perhaps acting on inadequate data, were beset by bad luck and bad judgment. They allowed themselves to be ambushed.

Some of their men were killed. A few of the wounded were removed, but others too badly hurt were finished off by their non-Gypsy comrades to prevent them from falling alive into the hands of the German police.

They were all poisoned with greed. My presence among the Rom suddenly seemed superfluous. The original vision had become tainted and perverted; despite my efforts my mission had turned into fraud. I lost all sense of personal accomplishment; I had reached a dead end. At first the Rom's participation in Resistance activities had seemed obvious and desirable, for the sake of their survival and to help defeat the Germans. But we had been seduced, small step by small step, into ignoring the price we had to pay. Had we simply been used as convenient instruments? In a way we had been utterly dispensable, we, the *Rassenverfolgte*.

Living under the constant threat of sudden death, some of the older Rom remained unaffected by the appeal of violence; some said that it was perhaps better to let oneself be crucified than to demean oneself by crucifying others. Old Bidshika said once, "They who see the sky in the water are likely to see fish in the trees." On another occasion old Lyuba, coming out of a daze, allowed herself to remark to me, in reference to our use of violence, something about "seeing lights in the water." The water perpetually flowed past and the lights were only reflections seen in it, which had no real, relevant connection. Rupa, who even more rarely commented on my unconforming ways, chided me about what she called my un-Romany admiration for The Hero. I felt the sting and knew her concern.

PART TWO

CHAPTER TEN

Like the insect fatally drawn to the flame that will devour him, I could not help myself from returning to the various haunts of the Tshurara and of those among the Lowara who had come to share their collective compulsion. Though I was fully warned of things to come, I was driven to keep in touch, to know the measure and extent of my failure to control the Tshurara rebellion against their commitment to the cause.

Kore kept close to me wherever I went, silently sharing in whatever I did, neither approving nor disapproving, faithful, inseparable, inexhaustible in his concern and patience.

Two days after the raid we went together to one of the blackmarket restaurants where some of the Rom used to gather. Pitivo and a few other Rom were drinking at the bar. Even though we repeatedly insisted we did not want to eat, they ordered and we were served a succulent meal. The lavish-sized broiled steak topped by fried eggs and the cool frothy beer made us relax, momentarily numbing my gnawing anxiety and smoldering anger. This exceptional meal reminded us of all the good material things there were to be enjoyed in different times. None of these things were available to the average citizen, who was happy to survive on boiled turnips, occasional potatoes, a slice of sticky, gray, indigestible war-time bread (made, it was said, from ground acorns), bad margarine, substitute sausage—substitute everything.

After the meal the owner of the place offered us on the house rare contraband Courvoisier cognac which I drank standing at the bar, leaning on one elbow, toasting our host.

Kore had left to go and wash up, when through the big plate-glass window on either side of the entrance with its double swinging doors, I saw several black cars pull up and stop short. Men in dark clothes jumped out and burst inside the cafe, arms at the ready. I felt oddly composed, fully aware of what was happening. As I coolly anticipated, they all converged around me, my back to the bar. The first one to reach me pistol-whipped me even though, to my own surprise, I offered no resistance. Before I realized it, another slapped on tight handcuffs which bruised my wrists. The inevitable had simply taken place. All superficial agitation died away. I felt very still. Only my throat and palate felt painfully dry.

The Germans rapidly fanned out about the cafe lining up the other customers, roughly searching them for concealed weapons. In their search they ripped off suit collars and tore open shoulder paddings of several people's jackets. They made several others remove their shoes for inspection. But none of the other Rom were either beaten or handcuffed. During the pandemonium an old lady, the mother of the cafe owner, with compassionate concern and unbelievably rare understanding of the needs of that particular moment, brought me a glass of water while braving the Germans' reproof. I drank avidly and it somehow resolved all my discomforts. The handcuffs were tight, but to my surprise I did not feel any pain from having been hit hard.

I was hustled out, pushed into a car, and driven off in a hurry. Kore had not come out of the washroom and for all their apparent efficiency the Germans had not searched beyond the main hall. Outside I briefly spied a shrunken human shape hiding his face, held up between two Germans. His feet were unshod and strangely swollen; apparently he could not stand unassisted. I wondered who he was. If, as I suspected, treachery had led to my arrest, it also held a troubling implication. We all knew of people who had died under torture. I had understood this intellectually, or thought I did. Suddenly I gained a visceral experience of it, though even now it was still an experience once removed. We drove off at breakneck speed. I felt old beyond my years. I was in fact twenty years old and ready to die.

We stopped at a crossroads where they transferred me to a waiting panel truck. I noticed several other prostrate, bloodied, handcuffed prisoners and I noticed incongruously that the truck motor was left running. I felt somehow reassured that I did not recognize any of the others. Several times black cars brought other prisoners. This must have been a prearranged collecting point and the raid an extensive one. I also wondered why it was made in early afternoon rather than at the proverbial hour before daybreak.

We were transferred to a large inner courtyard either of a police station or of a military barracks and made to stand several feet apart, to prevent communication, with our hands still in handcuffs raised over our heads, facing the gray humid wall pockmarked by bullets. At our backs stood uniformed guards manning machine guns. I expected to be shot in the back at any moment.

Instead I was taken up some stairs and into a small office. Ignoring my presence, a burly man with short cropped hair and dark civilian clothes was leafing through a stack of files. Expecting a far worse and certainly different situation, I stood wondering why I had been fetched. I became unrealistically reassured by the banality of both the place and the functionary, almost to the point of forgetting, for a split second, that I was a captive. I caught myself becoming irritated by the delay in acknowledging my presence as I watched his cigarette slowly turning to ash.

The German looked up with raised eyebrows and an unexpectedly conspiratorial mock-weary expression. Eminently conciliatory, he asked me if I spoke German and at my positive reply he heaved a sigh of relief. Most unexpectedly he reassured me about my present situation. He said that, in a way, my arrest was due to a mistake, raising my heartbeat to a mad tempo while breath choked in my throat. He stood up and walked over to me. He crossed his arms in a gesture of righteousness and looked at me with a theatrical and slightly sham benevolence; yet despite the elaborate attention and *mise en scène,* such as I imagined he might employ to win possession of a woman, I sensed an unmistakable menace in his attitude.

The National Socialist German people, he declaimed, were approaching the end of their heroic struggle and about to overcome the enemies of mankind. After this would come a well-earned Thousand Year Reich of law and order, peace and prosperity. Those who had fought for the good cause would be rightfully and abundantly rewarded. The forces of evil, and those who had sided with them, would be frightfully punished. I thought my amazed, angry, and stubborn reaction could not escape his notice, but his eyes remained glazed and unseeing. He went on to say that from my physical appearance it was obvious that I was of untainted Aryan ancestry and therefore deserved to be on the winning side, where by heritage I belonged. It was sadly true I had become entangled in a web of conspiracy and become corrupted and misled by association with these degenerate inferiors, those in the service of the Judeo-Marxist plutocrats. Yet, he said, he was willing to take upon himself, and he was empowered to do so, the responsibility for my rehabilitation, even though it was admittedly past the eleventh hour. To all this I listened in perplexed disbelief.

He would spare no efforts to induce my return to sanity, he said, but because he had become used to making threats he added, "before I surrender you to the proper authorities." The hint was unmistakable. "We know who the criminals are and we know where to find them. At this hour most of them have already been trapped. The chiefs have volunteered information and, while you are still trying to shield them, *they* have betrayed *you.* We know everything." And adding one more preposterous twist to his logic he shouted, "We, the Geheime Feld Polizei, will make you talk!"

I was hit on the mouth and the head and, as I lifted my handcuffed hands in instinctive gesture of protection, I was kicked in the groin. At the noise uniformed orderlies rushed in and, when he was through, removed me from the small office with a zeal and violence excessive to the obstruction or threat I did not even represent. It was part of teaching me respect for authority.

After dark we were transported to a nameless interrogation prison, a brick monster with hundreds of hungry eyes staring in the night. The cell was dark. In the otherwise hushed night I could not help hearing the intermittent screams of unknown people. On the outside, life went on. I was very hungry and cold. Deprived of sight by the darkness, I was assailed by the intruding odors of damp concrete and carbolic acid, stale urine and human excrement. Never before had my sense of smell been so painfully sharp. I lay prostrate in the dark a long time trying to avoid admitting that the touch of the sweat- and dirt-hardened cover of the thin straw-filled pallet, the comforts of which I could not afford to deny myself, repulsed me. I walked around my cell feeling the rough walls which were the physical boundaries of my world. It seemed already to have been an unmeasurable time span, an eternity, since I walked about town a free person, used public transportation, possessed private belongings. They took my belt and shoe laces. They contemptuously emptied all my pockets.

I wondered who else had been arrested and who had escaped the wide sweep of the scythe. What had happened to Kore after they took me away? Had they released Pitivo and all the other Rom who had been there drinking with us? I wondered about those Rom camping farther afield in supposedly safe havens, those in the woods. I wondered about Dodo, his wife Keja, and especially about their two daughters, Djidjo and Ludu, so vulnerable in their youthfulness. Had they been molested? I wondered about Mimi and her family. I wondered about Tshurkina la Lizako and Vedel and Merikano and also about the French safecracker Bernard, those rebels among us. The shrunken human shape held up between the Germans at the time of my arrest, whose feet were unshod and strangely swollen and who could not stand unassisted, reminded me hauntingly of young Djem, Tshurkina's son, even though his face was intentionally averted.

Hunger and fatigue brought about a confusion of thought

in harrowing obsessively repetitive cycles which, as the night wore on, I progressively failed to control or to stem. My imaginings were like the monotonous succession of desolate landscapes rushing past a train window on a long weary journey; I wondered at the still receding limits of my emotional endurance. I wanted to cry out, to sob, to release all the anger, all the despair, to go mad or just to die. Then came the self-lacerating "ifs"—if Kore and I had not accepted the meal Pitivo offered us, if I had abstained from drinking the cognac offered by the cafe owner, if I had not insisted on hanging around where the Tshurara gathered, if . . .

Then my thoughts narrowed down to my impending death. I had no illusion as to my personal fate. It was clear that I had been betrayed and as far as I could judge the extent of the raid proved a careful and thorough preparation based on inside information. It seemed to have many ramifications. I had not recognized any of the other people arrested with me, though they must have been run down in connection with our affair. I cursed those careless greedy Tshurara, and yet they were Rom like ourselves. Facing the same tormentors I could not side against them. That was the irony of my position. Acerbated by physical discomforts and fear, the sound of my labored breathing, the hasty beat of my heart, and the chasing of the blood in my ears and in my veins magnified to what I felt to be the aural physical threshold of pain. Suddenly everything was dead quiet again, and in a renewed flash of despair I knew I was in the total arbitrary power of those who had captured me, the Geheime Feld Polizei.

The hollow silence of the labyrinthine jailhouse was oppressive because I knew it was filled with muted, anguished, broken human beings, alone and desperate like myself. Through this night rose in ultimate defiance a distant but steady and clear voice. It spoke in Romani. I strained to hear but could not identify who it was. *"Romale tai Shavale, Tshurara tai wi Lowara"*—Responsible men and Gypsy youth, Tshurara and Lowara alike. It echoed through the hollow, terrorized place and I feared it would be traced to its source by the Germans and silenced before it could impart its message. *"Ame Rom sam"*—We are Rom, it said, in affirmation of Romness facing death, in a final appeal to reconciliation between feuding factions. Was he a Tshurari or a Lowari? *"Yertisar man tai te yertil t'o Del"*—I forgive you and may God forgive you too. The cry in the night was never identified, but it did not matter. It brought back to me a clear and strong vision of a long single line of Gypsy wagons and horses moving relentlessly toward the horizon. It was a vision of a floating world in a moment of timeless, spaceless quiet. Utterly triumphant in their refusal to abandon under defeat their preference for love, they were perhaps subject to another more exalted form of madness. They accepted the basic laws of nature and like all creatures of the wild were leery of traps. They were to be killed because they believed in freedom.

A flashlike explosion of harsh bluish-white and loudly resonant banging jolted me out of my dreams of peace. Through the steel door, against which he kept kicking to make the echo reverberate in my narrow cell, the night guard barked that it was *verboten* to sleep with my face hidden by the blanket. Spying on me through the small hole in my door he had to be able to see my face at any time. The light went out. I was alone again and all was peaceful. The reality to which I awoke after too short a sleep was worse than the most petrifying nightmare. Outside a new day was dawning. The twilight penetrated my cell through a narrow transomlike window. It was inaccessibly high, with stout close-set iron bars and, worse, a panel of frosted glass obliterating the small patch of sky I knew should be there.

But despite my sleepiness, curiosity about my new life and environment blotted out all else. In the growing half-light I discovered a dirty-looking three-foot-high metal container with a lid from which came a smell so foul it made me retch. Yet I was grateful it was there. Again I thought of my own destruction. I wanted to weep, to scream, but I couldn't. The outer shell of muscle, skin, and sinew seemed improbably frozen and indifferent to my inner turmoil. I was less frightened of death itself than being doomed to die barren, alone, and unheard. Nothing, no one would survive me, no child of my own, biological or spiritual. When it was too late, I understood Pulika's persistent concern about my taking a wife. It was like realizing hours, or days later, that I had seen something in passing I did not even know I had looked at.

Slamming doors, rattling keys, and the slowly rising crescendo of approaching heavy boots, rhythmically interrupted my whole being and echoed through the cavernous corridors. The heavy metal door of my cell opened with much clanging. *"Aufstehen, Schweinehund"*—Get up, pig-dog. This was a much-used German designation. *"Kübel 'raus, du Scheisskerl"*—Bucket out, you shit type. The German guard thundered the instructions. I dragged out the *Kübel,* in exchange for an empty one deposited before my door. The door slammed shut and the next door was opened. After shuffling of feet that door was slammed shut. The sounds subsided until all was quiet again. The intrusive cesspool smells of the new receptacle smelled different from the first one, the one I had come to accept. I waited empty of any thought and for a long time all was quiet. Then there was another big noise swelling and filling the hollowness of the corridors and the distant sound of *"Wasser."* After a long wait the footsteps stopped before my door and keys rattled. This time only a small panel in the door opened. Through it I hastily put out my metal washbasin to be filled with water. The panel shut and the footsteps slowly faded away. Eagerly I studied my reflection in the water before washing. I had no soap, no comb, no toothbrush, for that matter no toilet paper.

Bored and disconsolate, I paced the cell. Five to six steps one way, turn, five to six steps back. I walked senselessly, numbing my thinking. I started counting the steps and making up games. Uneven steps were good; even steps were bad. I attempted to adapt my strides to conform to my self-made rules about "good" numbers, in an all-too-human inclination to cheat even at self-made rules. As in gambling, there followed superstitious examination of these omens. Catching myself in time, I consciously stopped and rejected the senseless morale-destroying interpretation.

Through the panel in the door, which was always opened with great clanging noises, I received ersatz coffee and a slice of bread. The lukewarm coffee, the color of weak tea, smelled and tasted insipid. The grayish bread was spongy and difficult to swallow without liquid, but I was starved and welcomed the distraction it offered. The silence became sepulchral again and it was very cold. The light coming through the window seemed equally neutral and indifferent. It was February, 1943.

With a steadily mounting terror and curiosity I waited for the foreordained confrontation. Fighting with the normal instinct for self-protection, in anticipation of the moment, I desperately hankered to face the issue, to know rather than be forced to passively expect the worst, because more ominous even than the fear of death was the fear of prolonged unendurable physical pain. My anguish about it grew to ludicrous proportions, yet, I was sure, not beyond the abominations the Germans were practicing. I was unacquainted with extreme pain and feared it even more because of that. From the mysterious underworld of repressed memory surged a stream of weird unconnected images of torture and abominations: from medieval paintings depicting the martyrdom which had become part of Christian legend; from sensational headlines in the French popular press about so-called crimes of passion; from Goya's series of etchings on the military occupation of Spain by the Napoleonic forces; from fairy tales told in the nursery and which I had never before realized were essentially cruel; from Romanesque bas-reliefs and Byzantine murals representing the retributions of Hell; from the torments inflicted upon dumb animals by peasant children; from history and memories through the ages of the Inquisition, pogroms, and persecution; and from the special refinements of Red Indian lore in North America, read about and unforgotten. History and life itself seemed to throw up this bilious vomit of sadism. From later experience I was to learn that to maintain discipline in the face of death or under torture required a strict control of the imagination; it was the only way to survive in comparative sanity.

Torture was applied supposedly to obtain vital information. I had no doubt of what they could do, but I had not faced the issue bluntly enough before. There was, admittedly, no way to stop them from torturing me, but I was suddenly filled with the new reality of my moral commitment to protect others and the chilling new perspective opening up before me made me dizzy and filled me with panic. To die without betraying my companions still gave me a sense of worth, of meaning, perhaps of pride. The other alternative made both suffering and death utterly meaningless. The only escape open—escape both from unwitting betrayal under extreme duress and from fearful and vindictive punishment if one resisted—lay in suicide. In impotent rage I beat the walls with my head. When I came to, the silence around me seemed to have grown only more ominous and menacing than before. I could not shake off the heavy torpor, the numbing inertia. This was when they came for me.

The door blasted open. The guard stood before me very close. He knew the impact of his loud, blasting parade-ground shouting, and I felt like vomiting. We strode rapidly through long narrow corridors with endless rows of identical doors behind which waited caged men. Our steps reverberated, echoes within echoes. In the cold air the acid pungent smells of disinfectant and of male sweat gripped my throat.

We stopped before a massive iron gate. Keys rattled; it swung open. The guard on the other side let us in. We passed through the star-shaped nerve center of my new universe, the core itself of the sprawling prison buildings. Everywhere was the same heavy oppressive silence. Only the slamming of doors, the rattling of keys, and the footsteps of the guards broke the quietness. There were more corridors, more iron steps. A ridiculous, insidious little question grew in my fatigued mind: Shall we remember the way back later? I was irritated at myself for the stupidity of it. Sleepwalking must be something like this. What could the guard be thinking? I noticed earlier that he wore a wedding ring. How conventionally normal.

Loud steps rang out from the direction in which we were going and aroused my curiosity. From the opposite direction came another guard flanking a prisoner. They were still far away but my guard made me stop. He pushed me around one quarter turn so that I faced the wall and without explanation he pressed my face rudely against it. Prisoners were not allowed to look at one another, I guessed, to prevent possible communication between them. Another insidious little nonsense thought came to me: What power did they think was left to us?

They were about to pass us. I wanted very much to look at my fellow prisoner. Prepared to accept the consequences, I turned my head in his direction when by sheer inexplicable coincidence he did the same, taking his guard by surprise as I had mine. We were each slammed to the wall, beaten, kicked, and subjected to profuse verbal sexual insults. Beyond the immediate hurt, choking with indignation, I had found renewed self-respect affirming my human condition.

Arriving at our destination I undressed as told. My hair was shaved off. I passed under a badly regulated shower which alternated briskly from too cold to too hot. There followed what must have been a medical examination and I wondered why they bothered about such a thing. I was fingerprinted and photographed full face and profile, holding up a board with my new identity, my matriculation number as a prisoner. The room was big and the German police administration employees were bustling and efficient but not especially hostile. Even the guard with the loud voice and the quick fist who brought me here chatted in German with the others and seemed no longer to bear me a grudge. Together they talked about everyday, very human concerns. One related how on the black market he had gotten hold of two pounds of butter, half a pound of roasted coffee beans, and a fresh loaf of white bread.

I put on ill-fitting, scratchy, but clean prison garb and was returned to my cell to wait again interminably for interrogation and the torture I had momentarily forgotten about. The very smallness of my cell, instead of confining, now seemed protective, almost snug. The proximity of free human beings, even be they German prison guards or police administration employees, made me feel different and ill at ease, as if I now belonged to a different species and to a different world. I was after all, in their eyes (and they were the dominant majority), a dangerously aberrant asocial element, hostile to the new order, a subject who, through his subversive attitude and action, had degraded himself and fallen back to the level of a lower biological species.

The panel in my door opened and I took the steaming soup poured into my extended canteen. I squatted with it in my lap, my head bent forward over it, both my arms protectively embracing it to absorb the radiated warmth. There was a lot of soup, but it was thin, with just a little mush at the bottom of turnip and chafflike oatmeal, but no salt or other condiment of any sort. I ate hastily, felt too full of liquid, and sweated abundantly for a while afterward. Slowly I cooled off again and very shortly after that felt more hungry than before.

I became obsessed beyond all reason by food and hunger. I was plagued by the fear of total starvation. Indulging what Rupa called "possession by loss," I now vicariously savored my favorite dishes, those which I had failed to appreciate in the past because I had been too much in a hurry or too preoccupied with other things. In my new enforced austerity, and with the insipid aftertaste of unseasoned turnips cooked to pulp, I dreamed epicurean dreams. I remembered the highly seasoned cooking of the Rom, the roasted meats at the spit. I conjured abundant and varied feast-meals. When I tired of this, or when my imagination ran out of dishes, I was left only more hollow and nauseated with an unbearably increased appetite. Much later I learned this was a fairly common phenomenon among prisoners and had come to be dubbed gastromasturbation. They came to get me for interrogation when I least expected it.

I had heard from the far distance, *"Hundert und fünf, ins Haus"*—Number 105 (my cell number), interrogation inside prison enclosure. Lost in the inner world of the senses, I had not allowed it to connect. We marched through empty resounding corridors. I was terrified and ceased to think. The bleak end-less halls looked the same, but the direction in which we walked was different from that of the morning. We finally stopped before an ordinary wooden door. We entered a nar-row passage with linoleum on the floor. It was well lit and adequately heated. There was a smell of beeswax, tobacco, cooked food, and beer. From behind another wooden door came the gay catchy tune of a popular German *Schlager* mixed with raucous sounds of German conversation, punctu-ated, I imagined, by half-smothered shrieks of anguish and pain. The guard knocked at the door and stood stiffly at atten-tion. There was a special glint in his bright blue eyes. We walked in. I was pushed to one side of the room and down onto a seat. At ease were several youngish men facing an older one sitting on top of a table, leisurely dangling his feet. Their high black leather boots were shining, they wore fresh shirts, and their hair was neatly combed. They wore spotless well-pressed uniforms. The tableau was incongruously normal and, all evidence to the contrary, I still tried desperately to convince myself that such things as torture did not really happen.

On the opposite side of the room a naked man lay face down, strapped onto a narrow unpainted rack resting on wooden horses. For a second it evoked the image of a surgical operation. A man stood next to him and bent over him. Again I caught myself thinking of the "patient." He removed a soiled prop from his mouth and swollen lips and listened concernedly to the broken babbling, interspersed with panting and whin-ing. The other Germans drank beer and talked small talk. They looked so enviably clean, healthy, and whole, so smug and satisfied with their lives, that for a moment I envied them. The straps were loosened, but the brutalized body remained prostrated, shaking uncontrollably. Under the taut olive skin glistening with sweat, every strand of emaciated muscle stood out like an anatomy drawing by Vesalius. Like a pendulum insanely out of control, I went from detached clinical observa-tion to the extreme of human outrage, and then through insane terror to infantile inconsequential nonsense.

After a short pause the man was prodded clumsily into turning over into a seated position. His feet rested on the floor. Pushed by the shoulder and held up under the armpits by another German taking special care not to soil his uniform, he was gently taken out of the room like a convalescent patient. His feet were awkwardly apart and he moved in a peculiar fashion. He swayed and was unable to control the movement of his head. As he was taken out he lost control of his bladder and let the water run. Some Germans grinned half-embarrassedly. Another hit him on the head with a book he was holding, scolding him the way one would a child, repeating, "Keep it in, keep it in," to no avail. I averted my eyes more in shame than in fear. His mouth was open with slack chin. He made gurgling sounds which disintegrated in an attenuated explosion of inhuman insane laughter. He gaped with eyes empty of anything except lethargic fear. He looked demented or retarded, entirely disconnected, an idiot made so by his fellow men. From his appearance in its present state of distress, it was impossible to reconstruct who or what he had been before. Still, the Germans must have considered him important enough to have spent so much effort "persuading" him. They appeared unbothered, as if they lived on another planet and had nothing to do with it. They joked about some girls. They appeared happy and congratulated one another on some special achievement. They paid no attention to me. I was only an *Untermensch,* practically inhuman. Their laughter was boisterous.

I had managed to control the trembling of my legs when the German officer in charge of my investigation took me back through the narrow corridor with the waxed linoleum and through another wooden door into his office. There was a black plate on the door with his name and rank, but I could not read it in passing and it really did not matter—just a reflex from an earlier life.

I sat on a chair across from his austere civilian desk, no doubt plundered somewhere. He leafed through my file and looked up at me without hostility, but with a kind of undefinable bright stubbornness in his clear pale blue eyes. Lowering his eyes again he read aloud my name and asked me to confirm the information in the record with yes or no answers. At first impression my interrogator appeared reasonable, with a tinge of sentimentality, handsome and well educated, and unlikely to harass or torment me or to use torture.

I was impressed and also puzzled by the volume of my file. I wondered what it could possibly contain and where or from whom they had been able to gather all this. He read without making any further comment, but wrote copious notes on a blank sheet of paper. Interrupting himself in mid-thought he looked up to explain that he personally deplored the odious necessity of "that"—the torture I had witnessed—but it had somehow become a "required ritual" of this establishment. He smiled wanly. "That" had already acquired the quality of a discolored photograph. The measuring of time had become erratic and in its conventional form irrelevant to my experience. More happened in minutes or in a few hours than in months or even years of my previous life. Time had become syncopated, skipping whole beats, or alternating accepted rhythms. Twenty-four hours before was already a long past era, utterly unconnected to the present.

In reasonable tones my investigator spoke of our mutual interests. No doubt through an accident of timing and circumstances, our fates had interlocked. Without wasting time or goodwill we should arrive at "a simple accommodation" advantageous to us both. He was a member of the Geheime Feld Polizei; his duty was to bring the investigation to a successful conclusion, and he added, perhaps as a friendly joke, that he had no desire to be sent to the eastern front for laziness or inefficiency. By any criterion of self-interest he advised me to cooperate in order to avoid "that," to avoid for myself unnecessary "persuasion," as he euphemistically phrased it. What he proposed was temporary relief with no guarantee of his keeping to his part of the bargain, in exchange for my admissions. I saw the unfolding pattern. However, he left me no illusion about my ultimate fate—the verdict was made without trial.

I sat across from him accepting the comforting warmth, light, and cleanliness of the environment. With a strangely detached curiosity I mused over the fact that this man would probably be the last person I would see before I died. A great lassitude blunted my feelings. In the effective, deep-voiced, and best bedside manners of an old-fashioned country doctor, he advised me to save myself further torment. I closed my eyes and in thought heard Monsieur Henri argue that my moral scruples were escapism and that ultimately even the pure and uncontaminated, as he called them derisively, would have to resort to violence. And here I was face to face with the enemy and at the enemy's unconditional disposal. In a rising tone of high excitement I heard him say that it was the Judeo-Marxist plutocratic world conspiracy that "made happen" whatever it was that would happen to me, and to all those who had worked alongside of me and were locked up in this prison. He abruptly and angrily stopped his monologue, concluding with finality, *"Muss Ordnung sein"*—There has to be order. He asked me several seemingly unrelated innocuous questions. However much I tried to guess what he was driving at, I found them incomprehensible. I was uncertain of how much the Germans knew despite their boasts of having arrested everyone connected with our operation. I retained strong doubts.

Incongruously out of place, the image again flashed before me of a long line of Gypsy wagons moving ceaselessly into the horizon and into a new dawn. I heard Pulika remind me that "with silence you irritate even the Devil," suggesting speech as a more appropriate strategy to escape detection. I resolved to learn from the Gypsy women's fortune-telling technique; for so had said those who knew, "There are lies more readily acceptable than the truth" reflecting with intuitive anticipation what people wanted to hear. Only recently I had been unhappy about the Gypsy women's dishonest fortune-telling practices, even though I had accepted them for purposes of psychological warfare. Now I too saw the wisdom of lies. Pulika had often spoken of the necessity for the fox to think like the hounds in order to outwit them; and though they had run me to ground, I still had a chance to outwit them. I had to remember my Romness and revert to the ways of the Rom, learned in my childhood. I had to change the structure of my response. I had to induce self-wished amnesia, not to be unwilling to communicate—they will always attempt to break you—but to be *unable* to. I chose to remain inaccessible to their arguments, unprovoked, as Pulika called it. I would blot out of my memory ever having been an agent. J would need to hold back my compulsion for self-justification. I had to disguise not only my anger, but also my tenderness. I would be an echo, a shadow, a phantom, evading my condition, attempting by inventing, simulating, and counterfeiting to become invisible. I was party to the clearsightedness that extreme danger occasionally produced. The Rom said that "the heat of friction was a loss of energy."

My inquisitor looked at me with interest, but without the least suspicion, assuming I was thinking things over. What he urgently wanted was to make the disconnected fragments of the puzzle fit into a clear overall picture, to find and fill in the missing parts. I wanted to gain time, to weary him, to prolong my life at least for a time with a cocky determination to take, while giving in return as little as I could. I took my cue from the fortune-telling of the Rom, and after every involuntary straying from it I consciously returned to the same spot, gravitating again around the proved technique. As in fortune-telling, I must find the key to his particular echo chamber, for like most people he believed that whatever did not conform to his reality was imaginary and unreal.

Clearly he prided himself on being an efficient bureaucrat. He made a fetish of efficiency and had atrophied in himself the ability to learn from observing real life because it was more complicated than clichés or rules. For me it was a matter of learning quickly enough to speak his language, to use his code and answer his particular needs, with infinite patience and guile to scramble and unscramble meanings, to cover the essential trail with a wealth of precise dates, a profusion of trivial details. I sailed forth one day and with elation into an erudite dissertation on Gypsy grammar, the nine case declensions, reflexive verbs, syntax, and even semantics. I realized with satisfaction that he was bored but impressed, and at the same time that he could not afford not to listen—just in case.

As in fortune-telling, I threw in casual observations shrewdly calculated to flatter him, which surpassed in effectiveness any power to convince. I had to learn to control the slight breathlessness in my voice, though I soon learned that only I could notice it. Like an aspiring novelist, he plotted an elaborate fictional strategy which he then proceeded to flesh out from a voluminous filing system, in an obvious attempt to buttress his random, but fixated, hypothesis. Consequently any actual evidence was either twisted to fit a slot or rejected. There were occasions, though of necessity rare, when forgetting my personal plight I reversed the roles and pried out from him bits of information about himself. He had studied medicine and psychology, but because of the onslaught of the enemies of the Reich had joined the German secret police. Under the apparent exterior of drive, reliability, and thoroughness hid a compulsive emotional cripple, whose psychological instability hindered his ability to function adequately. However, this insight only served in the long run to warn me, rather than to shield me from his vindictive harassment.

The days and weeks ran together. The endless, monotonous, unrelieved agony and the grueling routine of daytime interrogation induced in me an intolerable, low-grade, but constant depression, with only occasional eddies of composure between waves of despair whenever I reached the limits of frustration.

CHAPTER ELEVEN

When I was left alone and did not expect to be interrupted, I found refuge from the desolation and emptiness of my existence by escaping into the past and gradually by projecting my intensified, secret inner life into a timeless future. In this havenlike isolation I talked interminably in Romanes, for though my thoughts could not be monitored I unconsciously sought the additional barrier of language as a psychological safety precaution in separating the levels of my thoughts. These lonesome night sessions functioned like a decompression chamber. I talked mostly with Pulika and Kore, only occasionally with Keja or with Rupa. At first I mourned for Pulika's people, this species about to become extinct and whose graves were to remain unmarked. And with them I mourned my own extinction.

One night a slight Gypsy tale came to mind about the *Brashki,* two frogs. It had been told to me a long time before by a little girl called Papin who was barely five years old. Rephrased and interpreted in my own words, it told of a good little frog, reasonable and well adjusted to reality, who, hopping around minding her own business, accidentally fell into a bucket of milk. Appraising the situation, she soon realized the physical impossibility of her jumping out again to save herself because of the size of the bucket. Accepting the inevitable, she promptly drowned.

The following day another innocent little frog made the same mistake and fell into a similar bucket equal in size and filled with milk. This little frog, however, was totally unreasonable, impulsive, and unrealistic. She jumped and jumped and never gave up jumping until the following day at dawn,

159

after having churned the milk into solid butter by her ceaseless jumping, she was saved.

With a smile semirecognition dawned, and I told Pulika that which obviously he knew—that though we were doomed to die we were still capable of wanting to live a while longer. Had not he himself admonished me once not to let the knowledge of death get between myself and life, to do as true Rom did even in the face of darkness: to assert joy. It brought to my mind the image of those small singing birds which the peasants kept in cages, blinded so that they sang ceaselessly in anticipation of a dawn which never came. Did not their singing make more, or at least as much, sense as weeping? Pulika had said to me, "I want you to love life more because of me." Now we were both to die at the same time.

In a daze of joyous amazement I remembered the last time I saw Pulika and felt he was there with me. By a circuitous route Kore and I had gone to Pulika's hidden camp deep in the countryside. It was still light and we sat by the open air cooking fire, as we had done before the war started. Through the quivering veil of flames I observed Pulika a whole and untroubled man. The unforgotten image acquired a density that had eluded me when it still could be touched. Djidjo had been there too, her eyes soft and wide with wonder. Unobtrusively, out of the corner of my eye, I had observed her body under the loose garment and her full long skirt. She was flowing with the promise of perpetuation of life. She had been hauntingly desirable in her primeval vitality, in the morning freshness of her body and her soul. At that time, however, I had been obsessed with war and death, devoted to a determined policy of harassment even if I had begun to have private misgivings. Absorbed in the fate of those working with and under me, I had been less concerned with myself. I had repeated to myself that there was no choice anyway. I deliberately had turned my back on the image of Djidjo as a symbol of life, which, in hindsight, appeared blurred as if by tears.

I saw Yojo's young wife, great with child and breastfeeding

another. At night old Lyuba silently covered my bare feet sticking out from the featherbed laid under the open sky, to protect them from exposure to moonshine so that my hair would not turn white prematurely. I saw Keja early in the morning tenderly gather the embers left over from the previous day's fire and blow them back to life to last another day. I saw the blossoming orchards, the swampy meadows. I remembered the rain, the wind, the sleet, the unseasonal snowfalls, and the yellow Gypsy dogs whining in the snow around the motionless wagons. And I was filled with love and tenderness, passion and gratefulness. I longed to achieve the Rom's inner freedom from circumstances: the freedom from superstition, the freedom to live and love, to be as they were (at least among themselves) without the need to pose. I longed for their capacity to find serenity within the conditions of life, forgetting starvation and outgrowing excess, and to rise above their outward fate. I envied them.

Talking interminably to Pulika and all the other Rom who were close to me, I felt the trust and warmth of their psychological intimacy; though naked to the violence of my oppressors and exposed to every arbitrary malicious indignity the jailers could with impunity commit upon me, I dared again to dream, as a supreme gesture of defiance, before the ending at dawn. Pulika had wanted me to love life. Because of him I still could.

My investigator could become violent over trifles. It was a severe winter and I knew from the days of my liberty that after their prodigious initial advances on the eastern front the war was going badly for the Germans. He burst out with bitter passion and indignation over the Bolsheviks' barbarity, treachery, and hate for the Germans. Overtaken by rage he shouted, "We will break them yet, we will wipe them out, we will show them who the *Herrenvolk* are!"

From time to time, either as a warning or a revenge, I was tortured. Pain came and went, and we resumed the wearying interrogation. Sometimes, remembering his interrupted medical studies, he would make private jokes by prescribing what he called some "purgative for my soul." Sometimes he contented himself by threatening me. I was never under any circumstance allowed to forget torture.

I was victimized by hideous waking nightmares which I could not stop. I was overcome again and again by a sudden disgust and lassitude, a sense of total ennui. We would be killed messily, destroyed, squashed like vermin and insects against prison walls. For what had we lived? For what had they lived, the victims everywhere? For what had they to die? In the face of senseless ugly death, what meaning could still be found in beauty, tenderness, hope, peace?

My stomach heaved violently and I vomited bitter gall and prayed I too could die, immediately. Why carry on? Why hunger for more? How could supposedly responsible men have wanted to love and to pass on life to others, to perpetuate themselves in their children? Why was it so difficult to surrender, to give up, to let go? Why was it that indignation at human injustice still rankled stronger than the longing for the final void? If it all had no sense, if I could not accept life, why was I equally unwilling or unprepared to accept death? If I rejected man, as I sincerely thought I did, why did I persist in seeing life through the very human convention I claimed to reject?

Between the two intentionally polarized layers of my prison existence (the exasperating, soul-withering investigation, the prolongation of which kept me alive though enslaved, and that of relating to the Rom) was an intermediary reality of day by day survival and the painfully slow healing of bruises and lacerations of the body.

Locked up within a narrow confined space, I was deprived of normal physical exercise and fresh air. At first I was held incommunicado. I was not allowed to write or to receive letters or parcels to supplement my badly insufficient diet. I was not allowed access to newspapers or books or any other sort of distraction from the unrelieved boredom. That winter I suffered from the constant damp and the icy cold of long nights against which I was insufficiently protected by my prison uniform and the inadequate single cotton blanket. Yet throughout that period I never had even a common cold.

Besides the bland monotony of our meager diet, in which both salt and sugar were totally absent, there was the constant pervading stench of human excrement to which, despite my hopeful expectations, I never became accustomed.

The hard rectangular environment was depressingly unrelieved by either color, shape, or softer texture. Concrete and cement were either left their natural gray color or painted a harsh bluish-white, dirtied by use and time; iron or steel window bars, cell doors, metal stairs, and galleries were battleship gray, and the rare wooden furniture an unappetizing shade of brown.

To keep clean we had an inadequate amount of icy water and no soap or toothpaste, no tooth or nail brush, and neither shower nor bathing facilities. Chapped hands or other abrasions and minor cuts infected and suppurated endlessly.

I wasted away as starvation caused my body to consume its own substance. My nails grew brittle, gums became inflamed and teeth loosened. In my very rare and strictly supervised contact with other prisoners I noticed, in contrast to our guards, how like old ivory their skins had become and how prominently their eyes and teeth stood out against their drawn emaciated features. The early morning stiffness of muscles and joints, also possibly due to "extreme persuasion" and beatings, was incompatible with my twenty years of age. Resulting from the combination of excessive deprivation and constant emotional exasperation, there was a near total absence of carnal desire. My sight waned and I often saw spots dancing before my eyes or experienced a throbbing sensation in which dim and overexposed vision alternated in strobelike effect. The walls were always a few feet away and I craved looking into the distance, to scan the horizon, to see extended perspectives. I developed an oversensitive reaction to loud or unexpected noises and overly bright light. My ears rang and I suffered frequent nausea and digestive troubles. I observed daily a slow, inexorable deterioration in myself.

I lost all sense of time, except that, on waking each day, I knew I had gained another reprieve. Transport to concentration camps and executions were by tradition before or at daybreak.

Daylight slowly lengthened and I knew that on the outside spring must have been coming, sap was rising in the trees, and seeds germinating as a new cycle of life began. The weather remained damp but was less cold. The low overcast skies, which I could not actually see through my opaque window, broke up and intermittently let through brightening rays of sun. When the skies cleared and the sun shone more steadily, I watched the reflection on my window of the passing clouds.

In addition to my daily concern was the possibility of being killed by an Allied bombing raid as I sat trapped in my cell. It was late spring 1943 and more and more frequently during the night I heard the siren in the city howling the air-raid alarm. I could hear the guards running to their underground air-raid shelters as wave upon wave of Allied bombers passed overhead. The German antiaircraft guns barked dryly and I could observe thin powerful rays of light sweeping across the restricted patch of sky in my window—like Pulika's Romani description of the sky mistakenly assumed to be the size of a sieve because seen from the bottom of a well. Some time later the planes returned, still pursued by ack-ack and searchlights, but the sirens did not howl because it was known that the planes had already delivered their loads elsewhere. My information about the progress of the war was limited to these observations. The Allies were now bombing more frequently, almost every night, and I was happy about it. Even though I would probably not live to see the Allied victory I rejoiced that one day the nightmare would be over.

At the most unexpected times several guards would invade my cell. Scowling and threatening, they searched and thoroughly scrutinized every conceivable hiding place. They tapped walls for suspiciously hollow sounds. They checked the iron window bars. They unscrewed the electric bulb and probed the empty socket for possible hidden objects. They forced me to undress, searched my clothes and my body. Having found nothing suspicious, they left, stamping on the floor, kicking things and banging the door behind them.

Once a week or so I was taken out of my cell and marched halfway down the empty prison corridor, past the row of gray metal doors of my section. Although I never saw any of my fellow prisoners, I knew I was part of a vast conglomeration. At the junction of several corridors and galleries, under the alert and close supervision of a German guard, I was shaved by a prison trusty. To avoid the slight possibility of contact between "politicals," the Germans infallibly chose for such chores criminal elements, as more trustworthy. I remember reflecting to myself with appropriate gallows humor that before his job as prison barber he must have been a carpenter proficient at planing wood. The rough scraping of the blunt open razor, without the benefit of shaving soap, left the skin painfully irritated.

While still on the outside I had been warned not to seek contact with fellow prisoners or to trust them, as quite possibly they might prove to be informers or even provocateurs. And except for gossipy intramural rumors, what could I hope to learn?

One night, however, driven by unbearable loneliness, I sought contact. I could not do so by tapping the walls. These were so thick and apparently transmitted so little sound that, except when taken through the corridors or with outside traffic when I was locked in, I could have thought myself entirely alone in the world.

Early during my imprisonment a Rom had called out to us in Romani, our secret language that hid us and gave us away too, and it had echoed at night through the darkened prison yard and reached me.

I jumped up, grabbed hold of the iron bars, and with difficulty—I was that weak already—I pulled myself up near the window opening. I imitated the call of the screech owl and waited for one of the Rom to answer me back. The electric bulb dangling from the ceiling of my cell burst into light and I was caught in the act. My first reaction was to feel deeply embarrassed and I let myself drop awkwardly to the floor. The guard yelled and cursed and pummeled me. Another guard came running as if I had started a mutiny. My arm was painfully twisted behind my back and, bent deeply forward, I was marched away to take the consequences. I was thrown in another cell. It was dark and even quieter than the other part of jail. I felt about in the pitch dark. With a feeling of revulsion I touched the *Kübel,* icy cold, damp, and stinking. There was no straw-filled pallet and no blanket either. I squatted against one of the walls, huddled up for warmth. I dozed off and slept badly, restlessly. I awakened in pain and waited. Endlessly I slept and awakened again and again, waiting for the light of dawn, until I realized that my new cell must have been underground and received no daylight. I waited and time stretched beyond anything I had ever anticipated was possible. I had the nagging feeling that days and nights alternated without my being aware of the rhythm. I was hungry, cold, thirsty, distractingly bored, and I was sure I had been forgotten by my jailers. I remembered a dark dungeon I had been shown during a visit to a most beautiful château, in which captives had been left to die. Surely I had been impressed, being still a child, but I had not been able to believe it and to identify with the unknown victim. *"Oubliette,"* the French guide had called it, and the long-forgotten word surged again charged with meaning. I also remembered being told that in their Christian concern for the prisoners, some noblemen had allowed one single opening directly to the castle's chapel to satisfy the condemned man's religious needs; after all, jailer and jailed shared the Christian faith even though the one caused the other to die of hunger.

I had heard about *dunkel Arrest,* the dark-hole cell, but I could not imagine that as a grown man I would be frightened by it in the least.

I completely lost all sense of time and because of this I became frightened to death of having been forgotten, and left to die of hunger. There was no *Kübel 'raus* routine, no ersatz coffee. Just silence and darkness. I tried to suppress panic. I tried to reason with myself. I tried to imagine the added

humiliation of the guards coming in while I was frantic with
senseless fear. I tried to relate to Pulika, to the Rom, to dream,
to forget this, until finally I jumped up and banged the metal
door and screamed for attention. Both were strictly *verboten*
and could only lead to further punishment. But terror of being
immured and forgotten was stronger than reason or fear. I
cried out in the void and nothing answered. I started counting
to estimate time starting from now onward, minutes, then
hours; after hours I lost track but went on counting. Despite
all my efforts I lost the sense of time to the extent of believing
my isolation had already lasted several days and nights. When
I had just about given up, a guard came, giving me a glimpse
of light along with a hump of bread and a pitcher of water.
The *Kübel* was not changed. The door was locked and the
sepulchral silence returned.

I deliberately and severely rationed my bread and water as
a means of dividing my day into periods and keeping track of
time. After what seemed like an appropriately long period, I
estimated that it must have been midday and therefore lunch.
I ate and drank and resumed my waiting until the evening
meal—or rather, estimated time of evening meal. But hunger,
thirst, and boredom still tinged by fear fooled me and distorted
my estimation of time. When I finished my bread and water I
tried to sleep until the next day. When I awoke again, I
thought to another day, I resumed the restless anxious waiting.
There was no hot soup or ersatz coffee to warm me up. Just
cold water and bread, and I was even thankful for that after
long enough a wait as limits of endurance seemingly receded
forever.

I was let out and the guard asked me how I had enjoyed the
last four days. That was all the time my indescribable ordeal
had lasted! I could not believe it. The hot watery rutabaga
mash was a feast, the bodily heat it helped to renew a blessing,
the neutral daylight a joy. I drank in fully the joy and richness
of everyday prison routine. I looked up at my narrow window
with the iron bars behind it and, as in a vision or a hallucination, I saw the dirty frosted glass pane metamorphosed into a
patch of unbelievably deep vibrant blue sky. The color and

intensity of the blue changed like a ripple over a pond awakened by a gentle wind. From the sky color it turned into the gentler tactile blue of a cornflower. It lingered a while until the surface melted into a liquid radiant blue in depth, yet intimate like the eyes of a girl I had known. It turned deeper still and more sensuous, the blue of the Mediterranean Sea, and then the darker mysterious Prussian blue of the Adriatic. I was elated and felt a sense of physical well-being spread through my whole body. I attempted semiconsciously to guide these experiences of color to red, because in a sense I liked red more than blue. Instead I saw the dirty frosted glass of my window for what it was, wondering why. I relaxed and the image slowly interceded. I briefly saw the red of gushing blood, and winced though the color was rich. Then another red, the color of fire; but instead of suggesting the Rom's cooking fires, it evoked the ravaging fires of arson and destruction. The sight of field poppies in the vibrating noon of a late summer made me happier. Then came the translucent red of wine. The red of cooked lobster made me tense slightly, but it was followed by the coarser red of the torero's cape, edged in gold, in the *arena de toros* in Madrid. The blazing harsh sunlight, the pageantry, the noise, the fiesta mood, the trumpets. Then came the bull, striated in red blood from the gaily colored *banderillas,* full of anger but doomed to die. I pushed away the image and saw in compensation the singing reds and purples of the stained glass of the cathedral of Chartres, glowing mysteriously in somber cavernous space. For a hesitant second I was aware of the universal cruelty expressed in the traditional Christian imagery of Calvary and martyrdom, but exposure to it had dulled its impact; only my present condition briefly revealed and renewed for me its message. The Gothic stained glass slowly dimmed to the glow of smoldering embers before disappearing completely.

On another day I unexpectedly saw as in an illumination the rich yellow of ripe wheatfields gently rippled by a breeze, and a glorious trumpeting burst of yellow sunflower. Then there was a large field of sunflowers, seen long ago somewhere in the Balkans. The leaves were black and shriveled, the stalks were dried out and crackled as the flowers ever so slowly turned to follow the setting sun. The field whispered loudly at sundown. The sundown turned into a deep gold before turning into purple. I saw the rich faded purple velvet of Rupa's skirt, the messy purple of wild berries on the lips of brown Gypsy children, and of the limpid amethyst mounted into a silver Celtic cross my mother used to wear when I was still a child, the purple of heather, and of the shadow of night descending over the Carpathian mountains.

On still another day I indulged in browns and blacks: the dusky, soft, healthy brown skin of a Gypsy girl; the same color brown changed richer and gleaming in the rain; the rich textured brown of a newly plowed furrow; the dark, silky, rippling skin of a stallion Pulika once owned; the brown of saddle leather worn and given patina by long use; the transparent brown of hot tea; the smooth shell of chestnuts. Then it progressed to the blue-black luxuriant torrent of Keja's long single braid, highlighted by touches of colored yarn with which it was tied. The color of a starless sky, of fresh black peasant bread, and of smoke and the shattered charred remains of a city violated by war. I deliberately broke off the sequence, only to resume another day.

I astutely induced the color white and kindled it with care. First the white of farmhouses specially whitewashed for Easter, of mist and lace and pearls, the white of a proud swan gliding majestically over the water at dusk, the throbbing white of molten metal in fusion, the hushed whiteness of virgin snow, the white of the shroud, the white of the surrender flag, and the white of dried and hollow bones. . . . I shifted to greens, gradually learning to master the technique of my particular kaleidoscope. I absorbed the lush palpable greenness of nature, the shimmering green of young leaves in spring, the luxuriance of meadows, of poplars, of spar, and of pine trees. Greenness expanded into an infinity of vegetative life. There was a last glimpse of green cucumbers and piles of watermelons seen long ago at the market of Sarajevo.

Years before, my father told me about a visionary landscape painter who had delighted in painting the most glorious sunsets. I believe my father said the painter in question was Turner, but the story might well be apocryphal though this would remain irrelevant to the deeper meaning of the tale. On a gray mild late mid-winter afternoon the painter sat at his easel working on one of his great sunsets. He painted oranges, vermilions, mauves, and purples bursting in all directions. A local farmer stood behind him patiently watching, incessantly shaking his head in disapproving disbelief until the painter became intrigued and asked him what it was that bothered him. The farmer solemnly declared that this was not the way the sunset before them looked. The painter looked to the distant western horizon. The sky there was dull gray overcast and the sun a minuscule livid lemon yellow disk. He was momentarily sobered by this objective observation, but when he looked back at his painting in progress he turned to the farmer and said, "Don't you wish you could see *that* sunset the way I paint it."

One day my inquisitioner took me to another large room in the interrogation section of the prison. There were several other German officers present whom I had never seen before. The officers bantered boisterously and ignored my presence. I was made to stand at attention facing them while another German officer stood up and said to me that he was my court-appointed defense attorney. He explained that he would plead Guilty in my name. This way the judges would "only" condemn me to death! I wondered at his cruel sense of humor.

I remembered wild stories about people taken to execution in the early morning hours, blindfolded and shot—with blanks. They were told: This was only a dress rehearsal! Or after submitting a prisoner to what was innocuously called the water treatment—either submerging his face in the water or forcing a rubber tube in the mouth to simulate the anguished sensation of drowning—the torturer would apologize, the establishment only served water instead of beer. In a conciliatory moment the inquisitor might offer to visit the prisoner's wife or girl friend after the execution to console her. If the prisoner winced, a score was made.

In a pedantic tone my supposed crimes were enumerated. I looked around for my inquisitioner to try and learn the meaning of all this, but I was sharply turned about by my "defense attorney." The military "judges" turned to one another with mock indignant whispers and promptly returned a verdict of death. My attorney raised his arm, clicked his heels and shouted, "Heil Hitler!" and I was hustled away bewildered, not understanding or daring to believe this had been the real thing. I tried to ask if this really had been a *Kriegsgericht,* but I was shouted down and jostled. I did not insist.

Back in my familiar cell I shook off the ridiculous notion, though their bad joke haunted me uncannily. I minded the disturbance to my self-made routine. When my thoughts involuntarily strayed to the possibility of my execution, my knees weakened. I felt humiliated at this lack of control over my own body. If I had to die, I wanted to be able to die spitting in their eyes, with braggadocio, with a show of final defiance and contempt, cockily refusing to allow my eyes to be covered by the traditional bandana. I did not want to have to be dragged to the wall unable to walk under my own power.

Soon afterward the guard brought a German officer to my cell instead of fetching me away. This had never occurred before and I could not at first guess the reason why. His bearing was military, but in an uncanny way I sensed a difference in his particular display of righteousness. He said he was the prison chaplain come to confess me. The haunting thought that a time was now fixed for my execution was unbearable.

I did not want to confess, not to him at least. I had nothing to confess, either voluntarily or under duress. If I had things to repent, I had done penance enough. I resented his pious manner and could only interpret his concern for me to mean the imminence of my death. Anger overcame fear and I flung in his face the abominations perpetrated by his people, by those wearing uniforms identical to his: the concentration camps, the systematic persecution of the Jews, the mass murder of the Gypsies, the ruthless elimination of all dissenters. His eyes darkened, but I could not at first make out if this was due to anger or sorrow. He denied my accusations without noticeable indignation. He said that of course, as a Christian, he deplored the odious exigencies of war forced upon the German people by "hostile foreign forces." Lowering his voice again, he repeated that he had come to give spiritual comfort to my soul, adding half in question, half in challenge, "You *are* a Christian, aren't you?"

I wanted to ask him to carry to close friends of mine an oral message, a farewell, but thought better of it and abstained. Impatient at my lack of response, he stalked away. For a time I listened to his heavy booted military steps receding in the void.

To judge from my heartbeat, time seemed to rush on at an accelerated pace, as if hurrying to be punctually at a fated meeting. A few nights later I woke up inexplicably moved by a premonition. I did not want to be overtaken unawares, to be awakened rudely for the last time. I had previously wondered, half facetiously, what I would be given as last breakfast. Long before I had read about and been somewhat morbidly fascinated by the idea of giving a man whom you were about to kill a fancy meal as a farewell. I waited, and as I had uncannily expected, I heard faraway steps coming nearer. As I knew they would, they stopped before my cell door. The keys rattled. The door swung open and I was blinded simultaneously by the light from the bare electric bulb in the corridor and light flashing on in my cell. I was proud to feel as controlled and unemotional under stress as I had for a long time hungered to be. I was standing ready to meet them. I was going to walk firmly and erect, without turning back once. Instead, the German guard pushed a young man into my cell and the light died as the door shut. The steps retreated. They had brought in another prisoner in the middle of the night. That was all. I collapsed and shook uncontrollably, betrayed, jilted by death, humiliated, and mocked.

In the dark I felt a steady hand on my shoulder and heard a soft voice address me in broken halting German. He repeated soothingly, *"Ruski, Ruski,"* and after a few words in pidgin

German he lapsed into a voluble flood of Russian meant to be reassuring.

Throughout the vast prison complex pidgin German had by necessity and for lack of any other common tongue become the lingua franca of the slaves of the Reich. The newcomer had neither pallet nor blanket and that night we shared my narrow blanket as well as we could. He was up at dawn and I observed him through my half-closed eyes, remembering the night I had thought to be my last. Why on earth had they brought him to my cell? In the conspicuous absence of a common language, he could not conceivably have been put in my cell as a provocateur; and in any case why would they have done that?

He was deeply tanned and had a broad open face and blue eyes. His hair was as blond as that of the Germans was supposed to be. Undisturbed that I did not understand him, he constantly spoke to me in Russian. Pointing at himself he had said repeatedly, *"Ya Rusky, ya Ivan Nicolaevitch Dolgopolow."* I understood that he was from Krasnodar, and I thought I understood him to say that he had been taken prisoner of war and had escaped and joined the partisans. Then I lost the meaning of what he said or perhaps I did not care enough. Most of his gestures—though they had the charm of unfamiliarity—conveyed no meaning, which surprised me for I had always assumed gestures to be universal.

The weather was warm, though I was constantly cold, probably on account of ill health, and much noise from the "outside world" penetrated the prison walls. When they passed the ersatz coffee and the bread through the hatch in the door, I received my one usual share but nothing was given to him. He only laughed. I still remembered being shocked at the unfamiliar sound of laughter. And softly, irrepressibly he hummed a Russian song in mocking challenge. It provoked an incredible outburst of anger from the guard. I tried to hush him but he made me understand gently but firmly that this was his moment of triumph. I shared my food with him, as the night before I had shared my pallet and single cotton cover. To the rage of the guards he sang the song of the Russian partisans, recognizable to those of our guards who had been combatants on the eastern front. When the cell door opened the next morning, he put the *Kübel* out for me and took in the fresh one. Ivan boldly pointed out to me a wide somber ribbon the German guard wore at an angle from his buttonhole which indicated service in the Russian campaign and said some taunting words in Russian that infuriated the guard. Despite a beating, Ivan only laughed his irrepressibly taunting laughter. The Red Army was advancing, he seemed to say to them, and whatever the Germans did the Red Army would win.

My peace was shattered. Ivan Dolgopolow talked incessantly, and when he did not talk he sang, and when he sang the Germans banged on the door and cursed. He insisted on teaching me Russian, "for when the Red Army came," and within a few days we "conversed" after a curious fashion. Then one night two new prisoners were thrown into our cell, upsetting a routine which had made me forget the reality of my desperate fate.

Unlike Ivan, the newcomers were issued spoon and canteen, pallet and cotton blanket. To my surprise they showed a strong dislike for my companion because he was Russian. One of the new ones told me he was a member of a right-wing resistance group, an admission which I considered ill-advised to say the least, since he did not know who I was. The other claimed not to know why he had been arrested, which, in a small way, showed some prudence and cunning. We were joined by yet two more prisoners. Six people now crowded into what for months had been my exclusive domain. They irritated me with their constant quarreling over almost everything from the sleeping accommodations to taking turns at walking up and down the cell or the use of the *Kübel*. The lack of privacy became unbearable and I longed for my previous blessed solitude. They had been arrested quite recently and griped continually about prison conditions and prison food and everything else to which I had long ago become accustomed. They had not been ill treated. From the outside they brought rumors about Allied military advances on all fronts and the increased bombing of German war industry.

All this left me full of wonder and with more than a tinge of sadness at not being able to share in the feeling of victory. Before I had a chance to adjust to my new circumstances I was moved to another cell with four other people, also new-comers. Every night convoys of prisoners came and others went. It was as if half the outside world was being brought in. There were shortages of canteens and blankets. We ran out of soup one day and simply skipped a meal. There was yelling in the corridors and others joined in singing Ivan's song of the partisans. At night the prisoners took to banging on their doors for hours.

One day before the midday soup I was fetched away and told to take all my belongings. We passed through the star-shaped nerve center of the prison and down halls I had never before walked through. I was given civilian clothes and some personal belongings that were not mine, but I saw no good in protesting. I was made to sign several forms, which I did uncomprehendingly. I would have signed anything they put before me. At this stage what would it matter? I signed with a shaky scrawl that nobody deigned to check and was marched away again through another part of the labyrinth to a wide well-lit hall full of people coming and going. Shackled pris-oners were brought in. I did not know what to make of all this, what to think, except that deep inside me something warned me not to dare hope. I was probably just being "taken for a walk," about to be shot in the back of the neck when lured on by renewed hope so as to offer the least resistance.

The prison gate opened before me. Still expecting to be shot "while attempting to escape," I remembered thinking that it would be easier to die in action. Outside the sun shone. The trees I had last seen stark and naked were a luxuriant green. "Normal" people walked in the street. I saw women and chil-dren. I saw a dog. All known entities, the shape of which I seemed to have forgotten. Without thinking any further I dashed outside the open gate and down the street with all the strength I had left. I mingled with civilians in hope that they would not shoot. People turned around and looked at me. A young prostitute put a protective soothing arm around my shoulder, trying to comfort me with a feminine familiarity to which I was not accustomed. With the other hand she popped a small wad of wartime money in my trouser pocket with a fast and experienced motion. Then she gently propelled me on my way again.

I was lost and did not know where to go, to whom to turn for help or hiding. I could not satisfactorily explain what I could not help thinking of as my "escape." Perhaps it had been an administrative mistake; perhaps they set me at liberty so as to follow me to an unrevealed contact. To what I owed my freedom remained unclear, and suddenly I feared my return to the world, if possible, more than I had dared long for it. I was sure that as soon as my absence was discovered the German police would be looking for me again. Instinctively I went to the poorest section of town, where my destitute appearance and my emaciation would be less noticeable and where people were more helpful and warmer. I ate and drank in a neighborhood cafe, still torn between the feeling of being hounded down and the bubbling hilarity at the sight of women and children, at the life and humanity I found endlessly diverting as if seen through new eyes.

CHAPTER TWELVE

I made my way to Brussels, where I contacted some Gypsies from the Sinti tribe with whom I had become acquainted earlier in the war. The Sinti were known as "German" Gypsies because they had lived in Germany for a long period. Many of them had given up wandering and adapted themselves to living in the big cities. In many respects they were totally unlike other Romany tribes. Their women and girls wore dark dresses, often of black satin, that reached to mid-calf. They wore almost no jewelry. When young their hair was worn shoulder length; when older, severely drawn back and tied in a bun. They were reputed to be sentimental and jealous, much concerned with romantic love intrigues. In general they were poorer than the Lowara, yet never went about barefooted or in rags. Their women never begged openly but sold lace from door to door. Again, unlike the Lowara, their marriages were not arranged by the parents and no bridal price in gold pieces was bargained for or paid. When a girl was in love and felt she was able and willing to support a husband, they eloped. They returned to their parents only after their first child was born. They were then publicly slapped and re-admitted to the group. The slap was symbolic or substantial according to the real feelings of the parents and parents-in-law. Among the Rom these marriages were said to be unstable and, reflecting the Rom's chauvinism, they claimed that the sexual mores of the Sinti women were not as strict as those of their own. The Sinti men and youth spent their days practicing the violin or the guitar or accompanying the others on the bass. Some were remarkable musicians. One of them, Django Reinhardt, was excellent and during his short-lived career gained international reputation as a jazz guitarist.

The family of Tikno unhesitatingly offered me assistance and hospitality with full knowledge of the possible risk. Tikno was a widower in his early forties with a sixteen-year-old daughter and five sons, the youngest of whom was still in diapers—or, Gypsies being Gypsies and in view of stringent wartime restrictions, their nearest equivalent. The household was held together under the supervision of the maternal grandmother, a formidable iron-gray-haired woman of diminutive stature who had a wooden leg. She had several grown sons and daughters; some lived in Germany, others in various parts of France. Those in Germany had received German education and training and had become integrated; those in France, despite the same opportunities, had opted for Gypsy life. Yet all maintained contact by correspondence and were loyal to the old woman.

That first night at the Sinti's I was afraid for them. If the Germans made a real effort to look for me it was only too obvious they would look for me there. Looking at the children I felt like a criminal. But where could I go? Whom would I not endanger?

My first substantial meal, in the privacy of a home and surrounded by warm concerned people and numerous affectionate children, was an unforgettable feast. We ate thick potato pancakes, sauerkraut, and a providential, heaven-sent pig's stomach. Afterward I felt a layer of grease harden on my lips and palate and a punishing heaviness in the stomach.

From Tikno and Poffi I learned the full extent of the successive raids on the scattered camps of the Lowara and Tshurara. The women and children, the old and the infirm, were dragged away, beaten, and kicked with senseless brutality. After summary searches for hidden valuables, their possessions were scattered and destroyed. As they were being driven off in open trucks, they had seen their wagons go up in flames, leaving them no room for illusions about their own fate. The raids had taken place in mid-afternoon. Many of the men had been arrested earlier in the day at various meeting places in the massive systematic round-up, the effectiveness of which could only have been made possible by up-to-date, detailed, accurate, *inside* information. The Sinti who lived in the cities had been spared. They had had no part in any of our "operations," either of the so-called "legal" or of the "independent" type. They had had no share in their temporary profit and advantages. Nor did they share the consequences on the day of reckoning. Yet they did not fail to respond when I begged them for help.

The Sinti had been exposed to German attitudes toward the Gypsies for a long time. They had been more accurate than ourselves in anticipating the Germans' intentions. One by one Tikno brought several other Sinti to the little house at the end of the dead-end alley where he and his family lived and where I hid out. Through them I made contact with members of two independently operating underworld organizations, one of which smuggled saccharine out of Spain. They were more evasive about their other activities, but left no doubt these were neither political nor anti-German, and therefore from our point of view reprehensible. Yet they agreed to help me, without asking any favors in return. Why they did so I never learned; at the time I was eager only to get out alive, to reach Spain, safety, and freedom.

I traveled to Paris, to Lyon, and then to Tarbes by impossibly complicated, roundabout ways and eventually I reached Pamplona without incident, where I was met and miraculously provided with a passport validated for my stay in Spain.

For a few days I lived well at a slightly seedy middle-class pension near the Puerta del Sol in Madrid. I did the rounds and stared uncomfortably at the other expatriate refugees and adventurers gathering at specific cafes. I ate too much, slept too much, drank too much, and soon became wearily disenchanted with what this half-conscious world had to offer. I felt conspicuously out of place. I contacted local Gypsies and with intrigues too numerous to relate I made my way back across the Pyrenees into German-occupied France, somehow committing the sacrilege, having once escaped, of returning to danger. With hindsight, I was to realize that in my despair I wished for death. I felt spent, empty, burned out. After a short euphoric elation, I had felt a sorrow beyond words instead of the relief I had anticipated. I wanted to turn my face to the wall and die. Returning again to the German-occupied territories was probably another way of surrendering myself to the void. I felt separated from humanity by an invisible wall.

When I returned I found out that Poffi and some of the children had been taken away by the Germans, not on my account, but apparently because they were betrayed by her grandson, who had been allowed to join the Hitler Jugend and had chosen in this way to affirm his loyalty. Being away at the time, Tikno had escaped arrest. Later he was joined by some of the children who had hidden and survived. Until the end of the war they disappeared among the slum dwellers of Brussels. For me this return was to be a total immersion in the ooze of war, waste, and despair. In relentless progression I learned about the arrests of Yojo and his young family, of Kore and Zurka, of Luluvo and his brothers, their families and dependents, of Bukulo and of Punka. I learned about the disappearance of my older sister Keja and her husband Tshurka, of Yayal and Paprika, of Nanosh, of Laetshi, of the annihilation of scores of the Tshurara, of my uncle Milosh recently escaped from the Netherlands, of old Bakro, and Finans. The pattern of disaster was all too familiar. I had returned to a worse desolation than my most wild conjectures had anticipated. The storm had come on fast. It had all happened already, unaccountably leaving me alive. From the scattered few who saw it happen but somehow got away, the news spread by word of mouth. From them I learned how those not quite quick enough to submit had had their skulls bashed in. The others were duly transported east to be destroyed later. Kalia had come back, his eyes empty of anything except lethargic fear; his mouth worked incoherently. Others who escaped urgently warned the survivors of the imminence of their own destruction, but with few exceptions there was little they could do as large family groups to protect themselves, and simply to survive as isolated individuals made little sense to them. The problem of each individual was swept away by the problem of all in the chain of mass murder, dislocating the rational structure of experience. We, the survivors, were condemned to live a fate worse than death—which must be lived to be understood—the delusional sense of guilt at having been spared, as if we had survived at the price of their deaths, by the betrayal of the murdered, the mutilated, the burned. Harder to accept was the guilt-ridden joy in living, simply because we existed, even when scarred by fear and hatred, while so many others were dead.

A hiding place had been arranged for me by a law student who until then had remained uninvolved in the Resistance. I was taken to the large country estate of his father, a conservative retired army colonel and widower who, because of his known attitude and past, was above and beyond suspicion of any kind. That night I took a bath, the first in more than six months. It was also the first time I looked at myself unclothed in a full-length mirror. What I saw reminded me more of a large skinned hare—as I had seen hanging from a hook in the kitchen at my aunt's castle after the hunt—than what I remembered myself to look like. The skin looked unhealthily bluish-white stretched over a prominent rib cage and a bloated belly, thighs and buttocks mere drumsticks. The ankles were swollen and were covered by runny sores. The face in the mirror was narrow with huge eyes full of somber mystery. The hair had grown back grayish blond. I stared at it lost in thought. During months of captivity I never had occasion to see myself, but I wished I could forget what I had just seen. I had become a stranger to myself. We stayed there together for about ten days. Because of the seclusion of the estate we could walk around in broad daylight unobserved and undisturbed. I read a great deal, looked at art books, and listened to classical music which dissolved my anger. We talked only when I felt like it. For a comforting few days I was allowed to feel again almost a human being. With rare concern for my need of privacy, he subtly lured me into daring to make tentative plans for "after the war." There were numerous signs that the balance of military power might be changing, and the phrase "after the war" was reintroduced into the vocabulary. He awakened in me a fleeting vision of a possible climate of compassion and dignity, of a world free of fear and want. I was unable to talk about my recent experience. The constant care lavished on me made me feel awkward and embarrassed. How could anyone expect me to find comfort in a world of desolation? I rested and gained strength and intermittently caught myself dreaming. One day I left abruptly. I made my way to Spain once more by a roundabout route.

My return to Spain, however, was once more incongruous and utterly unrelated to my life. I contacted the British and the American consular authorities, but I was overcome by an indescribable lassitude and sense of futility. Here was the freedom I had dreamt of a thousand times, but it had lost all savor. Maybe it was already too late, or maybe it never had been anything else but a dream.

Every night I had alarming attacks of fever, palpitations, and nausea, and I often suffered disorders of coordination. I slept too much. I was dazed by half a glass of wine and could not digest the rich Spanish food. I had had fantasies about this unrealizable freedom. I would eat in excess and drink in excess and do everything wildly in excess to retrieve lost time. Instead I lay in a small shabby middle-class pension in Calle del Principe in Madrid. I was deeply upset by the depressing masochistic images of a tortured Christ I could not avoid seeing all over Spain. I forced myself to go to the Prado museum, but art appeared to me mockingly irrelevant to the present—except for Goya's mighty *Quatro de Mayo,* his painting of the Spanish rebels at the *paredón,* the wall of execution, being shot by the French oppressors, the Napoleonic World Masters of not so long ago.

Sitting on a cafe terrace one day I was casually approached by a man who introduced himself pleasantly. At that time I inordinately prized my privacy, yet welcomed occasional contacts which I did not have the drive or urge to establish myself. With a conspiratorial air which immediately set me on edge, he rapidly added "intelligence officer" to his introduction. I half smiled, puzzled, but neither impressed nor pleased. He said "they" had followed my movements. Who were "they"? How did "they" know who I was, and why should "they" bother to have me followed? I suddenly feared their interest, their suspicion perhaps. I wanted at all costs to avoid having to explain or answer questions. I had been interrogated to distraction and I would rather die than have to justify one more thing. At the same time I was sarcastically amused at how easily, in the relative safety of Spain, he had introduced himself in the capacity of intelligence officer. All I wanted was for them to leave me alone, and at the same time I realized how impossible a wish this was. But then again it could be far less cloak-and-dagger than at first I had thought; I had voluntarily contacted British, American, and Belgian consulates, and all that happened was that some of these elusive intelligence officers had gossiped about me unsuccessfully. What reason did I have to trust them?

It was his turn to smile, and before I had a chance to disengage myself he made it clear that all "they" wanted from me was that I help set up an "independent" escape route between Germany and Spain. With no questions asked and plentiful financial means, my services would be limited to two or three months at most, after which I would be called back to England for a long and deserved rest. I instinctively pleaded ill health, which was visible enough, and the fact that I was known to the German secret police, yet he had no great difficulty winning me over to the proposition. Like an old man deprived of responsibility, I had been restless and dissatisfied with my freedom, which in the middle of war meant inactivity or uselessness.

I learned that the life expectancy for an active network of this sort rarely exceeded three months. Escape routes were in fact a kind of glorified travel agency and by necessity they had many more extraneous contacts than any other underground operating group. Unavoidably we became known to the numerous people we helped across to Spain on their way to England or the U.S. Though we took great care to avoid detection, even by sowing contradictory clues, we left a detailed trail of vital data about ourselves and our mode of operation. As our "clients" reached safety they talked about their escapes among close friends or within the restricted circle of the service; but gradually the talk filtered back to German intelligence. Not for nothing were posters displayed in England warning that "the enemy is listening." Subsequently I was to learn that some earlier escape routes had been cleverly infiltrated by the Germans, who permitted the organization to function "normally." However, the Gestapo reserved for themselves the privilege of first choice whenever important persons or irreplaceable specialists were being "exfiltrated." Somehow the mishaps could always be explained later, and afterward everyone was only too happy that service could be resumed, instead of having been totally destroyed.

I left a few days later with several important contacts in business circles all over German-occupied Europe. The problem was that all of these had to be memorized. I was provided with ample money, false identity papers, and an adequate cover story. I felt reborn, cleansed of cumulative frustration. I could again enjoy a sense of adequacy and intoxicate myself with action in order to escape limbo.

I crossed the Pyrenees back into hell.

PART THREE

CHAPTER THIRTEEN

I went to Paris and Brussels. In both places comfortable, indeed luxurious, quarters had been put at my disposal. I acquired a new set of clothes on the black market. Breaking radically with my past, I affected a rather elegant suit, striped silk shirts and a flashy silk tie. With this I wore extravagant pointed yellow patent-leather shoes. My hair was dyed dark. I became a different person. At first I circulated at will with a false Swedish passport and as a cover I had a semiofficial function, but I did not speak Swedish and I constantly dreaded meeting a German who could. At that time I felt an almost superstitious compulsion not to hide from anything. With a show of recklessness that soon became part of my new identity, I escaped notice of the Germans because it was inconceivable to them that anybody trying to hide would dare to show himself as I did.

I lived surrounded by comfort and luxury and grew accustomed to believing in my new identity. For a while I found an escape of sorts in my fictionalized identity where to simulate was to invent, yet sometimes in contrast to my outward appearance of restraint, indifference, even of sophisticated boredom, I felt a recurring and frightening turmoil, a search for coherence, for meaning, a hunger for psychological intimacy in violent reaction to the calculated deception forced on me. I abhorred the pressing necessity to build relationships solely on the basis of convenience and necessity, evaluating men by the function they could fulfill and the services they were likely to render when the need arose.

I gained weight and my health improved, though the weight I gained was unhealthy fat which puffed up my face. I depended on daily injections to keep me going and frequently suffered attacks of high fever. Whenever I could afford to do so, I spent a few days at my bachelor's quarters. I read or listened to classical records and occasionally listened to the BBC. But because of my still shaky nervous system, I found this either too exciting or at times uninspiring and remote to our pressing problems of survival.

Most shops were shuttered and deserted. At many private residences curtains remained drawn. Cats and dogs had to a great extent disappeared. Electric and telephone services were sporadic and there were queues everywhere and for everything. The city buses operated on wood- or charcoal-burning "gazogene" tanks that weirdly changed their appearance into that of clumsy giant beetles.

Disturbances of varying intensity erupted everywhere. The Germans imposed new and more stringent curfews and there were checkpoints and barricades everywhere. The Germans were becoming hemmed in on all fronts, but boasted louder than ever about the secret weapon that was being perfected which would bring them final victory.

I was oblivious to everything except supervising the organization of our new *filière,* our escape organization or underground railroad. Part of my mission was to link up a number of unconnected networks limited to specific national territories into one large-scale, overall route between Germany and Spain. Most of the "fronts" through which we worked were respectable business agents and bank officials. Many of those working with us had been waiting out their time while more impulsive or enthusiastic elements had been gradually eliminated by the Germans. The entire operation was most professional. The relays or temporary hiding places were mostly in urban centers, taking advantage of the facility there to maintain anonymity. They were organized by people with official covers, such as functionaries of the National Food Distribution Office or the Post Office Workers Association. By this time even a number of people who worked in association with the German occupying forces and anticipated the possibility of an Allied victory started to take out "fire insurance" by cooperating with the underground. They were highly valued, whatever our moral reservations about them.

I raged against physical limitations imposed by my health, and facing a new challenge I sought to develop new techniques to economize on expenditure of effort. One day we hit upon the preposterously bold idea of simply posing as German recruiting agents for Organisation Todt. This new strategy permitted us to transport six to fifteen men at once, using the direct long-distance transportation of the German military through trains and German travel warrants. The necessary forms were in due time procured in quantity through Sinti girls I knew who, having "passed" as German citizens, worked in official capacities with the German military administration. All we had to do was fill in the forms, making sure that the dates were correct. The function of the German military police was to check on the dates on all warrants issued to Wehrmacht personnel and to all others actively engaged in the war effort. We "attached" ourselves to the *Hoch und Tiefbau*—what the Allies referred to as the Atlantic Wall and which included such things as U-boat shelters—in the south of France, conveniently close to the Spanish border. The Germans had created a thirty-mile restricted zone parallel to the Spanish border. Crossing this area was difficult and in order to avoid establishing a recognizable pattern we had to change our technique constantly. At the foothills of the Pyrenees our recruits were taken over the mountains by hardened professional smugglers. It was an arduous climbing trip of from ten hours to three days, depending on various circumstances. The shorter routes were used less frequently and kept in reserve for priority cases. On the other side the group was met by a reception committee who took them in charge.

All this had taken slow and thorough planning and required the active participation of far-flung carefully interlocking expertise. The recruitment of "candidates" and security checks were done by special local committees in charge of specific "retrieval zones." They also provided temporary hiding places for those chosen. The local groups had no way of reaching those in the next echelon, who kept informed and collected the "passengers" as soon as the next "station" was cleared and ready to receive them. They were then taken to a city hideout where they were outfitted and briefed. Then they waited until the "line" ahead was cleared for their transportation. In order to avoid awakening suspicion, the same hiding places, or *planques,* could not be used too frequently. The necessary travel orders were prepared and the great trip, the "tunnel," could be undertaken. At the Pyrenees they were given mountain-climbing boots with heavy spiked soles. For obvious security reasons, such suspicious gear could not be carried along in one's personal luggage. These boots, difficult indeed to obtain in wartime, were worn over layers of wool socks to adjust the fit. We also provided woolen sweaters and short sheepskin coats for the trip; two pounds of sugar cubes, one pound of smoked bacon, and a flask of brandy for sustenance and added protection against the cold.

The escape route functioned for several months without any noticeable mishaps or any suspicious events. Then a young Dutch banker who had come to Paris on official business had me come to meet with him at the Hôtel Georges V. He informed me that "my aunt was sick," warning me that something had gone wrong with the organization. He did not have an opportunity to explain, but it was clear that we had to disband, to melt away leaving nothing behind. There was no point in holding on. Unfortunately, he was sure that my aunt would not live. I left hurriedly in inner turmoil. As far as I could judge everything was functioning normally. The elegant Hôtel Georges V, his, and my own impeccable appearance seemed to indicate that all went well. He had slipped me an envelope containing what I later discovered was a substantial amount of extra money in various currencies—"to take care of the hospital bills," he had said.

At that moment nineteen people were in hiding in greater Paris, waiting to be evacuated. We decided to take a wild risk and attempt to save whomever we could on a last mad escape. If our mode of operation had been discovered, it would no longer be safe to use the convenient German military travel warrants or any of the rest of our established paraphernalia.

We managed somehow to have false French identity cards made out for us and fitted with the appropriate photographs, as well as other necessary travel permits for our last batch of fugitives. They were supposed to be French citizens originally from the Tarbes, Lourdes, and Mauléon vicinity in the *département* of the Lower Pyrenees, volunteer laborers working in the German war industry returning on a ten-day home leave. We were to travel by regular French civilian trains, which were a slower means of transportation than I had become accustomed to. They were also "controlled" more often and more thoroughly, but we had no other choice.

After getting everybody assembled at an artist's studio in Montmartre (we threw a small party to cover the unusual traffic), we left that evening from the Gare St.-Lazare. We had hastily gathered enough odd clothes and other personal belongings to provide each one with some luggage, battered cardboard suitcases, packages tied with string appropriate to a *Lumpenproletariat* of sorts returning home for a brief furlough. We were a disparate group and to my distress as un-French looking a bunch as possible. For once I had not had time to become acquainted with them beforehand. Among them were three Americans, an Air Force captain named Bill Utley, a radio man, and a heavyset taciturn operative; two Britishers, a Canadian bomber pilot, four tall Dutchmen, and a number of Poles. We spread out throughout the train. It was cold and humid. A fine rain had fallen continuously since daybreak. I turned up the collar of my wet overcoat, undid my shoelaces, and wedged myself in my seat, letting my ears and head be filled with the rhythmic sound of the train. In the gathering night everything was gray and drab and my body pleaded for sleep. Our attempted flight seemed doomed to failure. I felt my end so close at hand that for a tempting moment I was inclined to care no longer about the others.

I was awakened for the first control, either to check our railroad tickets or travel permits, whichever. I followed through automatically without completely waking up. There were several more similar checks and since no great commotion occurred on the train I guessed that sheltered and disguised by a similar combination of sleep, cold, and inertia all the others had also "passed." A disquieting echo arose from the recesses of my memory, humorous in a way, yet ominous in the present circumstances. A man I knew had attempted to pass cunningly disguised as a Catholic priest. It had worked like a dream and he had been shown subdued concern and respect as a "man of God." However, seeing a beautiful girl he momentarily forgot his vows of chastity and with behavior unbecoming to Catholic priesthood he had appreciatively looked her over. He was promptly arrested and held for the "further investigation" of his identity papers. I remembered other men I had known who mistakenly, but with a touch of middle-class romanticism, disguised themselves as workmen in overalls and rugged working shoes—everything a disguise should be. At the first checkpoint their clean fingernails and uncalloused well-cared-for hands immediately gave them away.

Throughout the night and the day that followed I heard the plaintive hooting of the locomotive as we passed cities and villages. Ever so often we passed intimate and gentle-looking burial grounds where, in contrast to our mad way of life, even death seemed friendlier and more human.

Our train crawled and frequently was shunted to let pass express trains carrying German military personnel or war matériel. People took advantage of these unplanned stops to get off and stretch their legs. As time wore on we acquired an unwashed, unshaven, red-eyed appearance.

In the afternoon we left the train at Tarbes and after I failed to make contact, we took a bus to Lourdes. There we were warned away. We started for Mauléon. I had the distinct feeling that everyone was watching us and knew who we were. It was impossible to loiter much longer without attracting the Germans.

Night fell and for a short moment I felt protected, though I knew nothing really warranted this. Three women detached themselves from the surrounding darkness and walked straight over to us. They were wrapped in dark shawls held tightly around their shoulders and arms. The youngest one hid the lower part of her face in a coy gesture of feminine modesty. They simply said "the men sent us." Too tired and dazed and desperate to question or to be surprised, I followed them and the group followed me. Soon we split three ways and disappeared under the cover of dark and rain. The dénouement was explained to me later by a Resistance liaison operative as not altogether altruistic. Since the entire region was already in turmoil, there was no reason to heighten the Germans' suspicion and ultimately their wrath by letting us blunder into their hands. I was still suspicious that his friendship might mask his intention to deliver us to the enemy.

A young Dutchman and myself were staying for the night in the house of the operative's mother. She was a nice old lady and I guiltily realized the risk they were taking in hiding us, for unlike the majority of them I had known jail and jailers. The two of us shared a large room on the second floor with a huge double bed in the middle. Showing us to our room, the old lady had made a point of telling us the sheets were clean, though old, and that this particular bed had often been used by British pilots escaping to Spain. She said it as if trying to reassure us that all would be well.

The wind was changing and outside the wooden shutters were slapping against the windows, making the panes of glass rattle in their frames. There was a stale, but by no means aggressive, smell of a small country town hotel—the smell of ancient dust, like that of old houses when they are being demolished, mixed with the faint odor of wet rags and a light whiff of outhouse and cooked cabbage. For me these were forgotten smells and I wondered why they were so hauntingly familiar, as if they were pretended memories to match my adopted identity.

I undressed and, as I had become accustomed to do, laid out my shoes and clothes so that I could slip into them quickly in case of emergency. I lay down between the rough musty sheets. From a light dozing I was awakened by the staggering motion of a speeding train. Afterward I could not sleep again and lay listening to the long-drawn whistle of a locomotive shunting at the depot and the urgent restless rattling of the shutters. It had been a taste of rest but surely not enough to keep me going. The unknown Dutchman slept next to me and I felt very alone, with the random solitude I had known in railroad stations the world over, full of bustling unknown people, the solitude of cinemas and restaurants and hotel lobbies at the early hour of anonymous departures, the solitude of places where one had once been happy.

CHAPTER FOURTEEN

In the past my contacts in the region had been with mountain guides and our arrangements with them had been strictly for cash. The price had to make it worth the risks for these hardened life-long smugglers. On their way back from Spain they smuggled goods for their own profit. I found that saccharine was very remunerative.

Some guides not affiliated with established escape routes had been known to take money from unwary stragglers who had made their way to the Pyrenees on their own and at unbelievable risks. The fugitives were then turned over to the Germans for an equal price and at no risk, and the criminal guides made a double profit. A believable threat of retaliation had to be projected to make sure of the guides' continued services and loyalty. To carry this off convincingly often took ingenuity, guile, and the straining of my inborn inhibitions.

The following day one of the women and her young son came to guide me. Her presence and that of the child served to better integrate me into the local scene. Several old-time smugglers, whom everybody knew and respected, had been arrested by the Germans within the previous forty-eight hours, so everybody who had been known to be involved in various aspects of smuggling wanted to lay low and wait out the storm. Here we were, nineteen fugitives, and I knew it was not in our interest or that of our hosts to wait around for safer times.

We met with mountain guides and tried to make them change their minds, but knowing the odds, all shied away. I pleaded. I offered to double the usual price per person from 10,000 French francs to 20,000, but to no avail. In exasperation I threatened, but they knew too well I was only gambling from need. I challenged them and flattered their sense of pride. I worked on their sense of guilt until even I feared I had gone too far. They might have been tempted to eliminate us, to betray us in order to exonerate themselves or to gain possession of the large sum of money I had been forced to admit we had. It was time to move on—anywhere. All my reserve of resilience, courage, and self-assurance, accumulated from months of successful operations, had faded away. There was no way out, except, perhaps, in the open mountains, streaked with their patterns of snow which altered daily and where the higher peaks were still lit by sunlight, beckoning above the formless immensity slowly being obliterated by the gathering night and mist. I was fully aware that this sudden urge to simply take everyone out in the open was the ultimate madness.

We returned to the previous night's lodgings where I had left my Dutch companion who, having feared my desertion, nearly cried with joy when he saw me. He was the only one aware of my discouragement and of my fumbling fruitless efforts.

The old lady prepared a savory cheese omelet with roasted potatoes and insisted we both eat before leaving. Neither of us was hungry and we did not know when we would leave or where else we could go. In any event, we had to collect the seventeen others before even thinking of a senseless plunge into the dark.

It rained and the wind kept blowing, and it was cold.

The old lady volunteered that she had spoken to both her son and her son-in-law, who had promised, if nothing else worked, to try and help. They would take us into the mountains. The son-in-law had a truck, some gasoline, and also a permit from the Germans permitting his circulation. He would be driving to some mountain hamlet to collect a load of cut firewood, and he was willing to take the risk of bringing us at least part of the way. She seemed relieved when I told her we had a sum of money set aside to pay off whomever her son and son-in-law considered advisable to gain to our side, provided they were willing to handle the matter for us.

In an hour and a half we were on our way. I sat next to the driver. My papers were in order and, unlike the others, I spoke French perfectly. I was anxious to see what would happen, even though I knew that in a real confrontation there would be little I could do. The others lay in the back of the truck under a large tarpaulin held up like a tent by some sacks of potatoes and various odd boxes.

Only once on the way up did two French gendarmes standing by their bicycles wave powerful flashlights at us to make us halt, but without even slowing down the driver leaned out and yelled at them something I could not understand. They let us be, though for a moment I expected them to shoot at us. I looked at our driver, but he only smiled and said cryptically, *"Ceux-là"*—Those over there. Everything was going well, but I could not completely set aside my distrust. It was going almost *too* smoothly. I feared it might be just a cleverly set ambush, but I had no choice but to wait and let him drive us to a destination which only he knew.

The steeply climbing road twisted in hairpin curves and the air seemed cleansed by the cold, the altitude, and the continuing drizzle. Observing him closely I suddenly sensed his growing tenseness. He stopped the motor, half opened the door, and leaned out of the cab. Through the still mountain air came the faint whine of motorcycles. He jumped down, ripped off the tarpaulin, and urgently motioned us all to run and hide away from the road. As we ran up the slope we heard the open truck roar on its way and disappear around a bend. We ran on in complete disarray, directionless, overtaken by panic. When we were out of breath we collapsed on the muddy ground and listened. The night was unusually astir with road traffic. The Germans must have been alerted. A German military vehicle with its lights on passed on the road we had just left and we could hear the excited barking of wolfdogs trained to hunt down and attack humans. But the truck passed. Driving by in the night with their view obscured by the rain, they had obviously missed the messy telltale trail of numerous feet clambering over the low stone wall flanking the road, signs which in our haste we had carelessly left behind and could no longer erase. The effectiveness of police dogs only began from the moment the first scent was picked up, and for now they had bypassed us. Their oversight in not spotting our trail corrected ours in being careless enough to leave one.

We got up and moved on over the rough terrain, occasionally splashing noisily through the mud of swamped meadows on the southern slope of the mountain. It occurred to me that we did not even have a map of the region, although I knew it could not do us that much good. We needed a guide. Rain trickled down our necks, our clothes were soaked and mud-covered, our feet were cold and wet. The Poles were the first to become aware that something was wrong. After some low-voiced discussions among themselves, one of them came to me. He said they knew but the others did not, and as long as they didn't we should hide from them the fact that we were lost lest they panic. I should display firmness and they, the Poles, would back me up. We kept climbing through rain and wind, to which half-melted snow and sleet was soon added.

At the end of a long climb we found ourselves among some gnarled old fruit trees and beyond this we discovered a mountain hut. We stopped and made everybody lie down. Unasked and of their own accord, two determined Poles followed me to the hut. As we approached a watchdog barked and strained against his chain. The low door opened and, outlined against the light of a candle or lantern, we saw a woman of undetermined age. She yelled roughly at the dog as I alone came nearer. She stood leaning on a wooden pitchfork, made from a forked branch of a tree stripped bare of its bark, and she gazed at me unblinking and unafraid. She was gauntly handsome, but her neck was disformed by a goiter. I tried not to frighten her, not to make her feel threatened or startle her by the loudness of my voice, and I prayed the others would not reveal their presence at a wrong moment. I explained to her that I was lost. I added that I had some companions along a little way down. We did not want food, neither did we want shelter, all we wanted from her . . . The dog started howling again and this time to my chagrin she did not try to silence him. Above the wind, above the barking, above my growing anxiety I shouted all we wanted was for her to indicate the way to . . .

I was shoved hard in the back. A man stood two steps behind me poking the barrel of a carbine in my side. Then there was a commotion and the man lay suddenly spread-eagled on the ground face down and the dog nearly choked himself pulling on his chain in his desperate try to assist his owner. The man must have come out of the hut when the dog first started getting restless and had hidden in the dark near the rabbit hutches. But he had apparently not anticipated the cunning of my two Poles who had remained hidden behind the stack of newly cut logs and had seen him checkmate me. The woman stood still and, lifting a hand gnarled by rheumatism, told the man something I could not follow. The Poles released their grip; the man got up. He shrugged and went inside, motioning me to follow, but the woman unexpectedly barred the entrance to the two others in a display of authority which they accepted without protest. Ignoring her, they said that if I needed them they would be there waiting and that they would take care of everything. They sounded properly ominous, yet somehow the tension rose again and made it difficult for me to ask for help and advice. Surely we could, if we wanted, force him to lead us, but as the Rom said, "Those who are forced to go to church pray badly." He could outwit us in endless ways. We could keep his wife as a hostage. But before I lost myself in more labyrinthine conjectures, he asked, in a manner less unfriendly than I anticipated, what we wanted him to do for us. His tone was just the habitual gruff tone of those who lived for long stretches of time isolated from their fellowmen, surrounded by these overwhelming mountain ranges. He showed no ill will about the treatment received, and, nodding toward his carbine leaning against the wall near at hand, he said vaguely, "These days one never knows. Better to be prepared."

In short, he agreed to take us to Spain. It would not be an easy trip, he said unpleasantly, but reassured by his ready acceptance to help us I did not take undue offense at his complaints. I wanted to allow him to save face.

He took a sturdy gnarled walking stick from a corner, slung a haversack over his shoulder, and without addressing a word to the woman, simply opened the door and left. It occurred to me that he left his carbine behind for the woman's safety. The Poles emerged from the darkness and without any further exchanges between us we joined the others.

Waiting for us they had grown cold and wet. They stumbled up when we came and formed a single line to follow the guide. He had squinted at the sky and after a short pause said with a grin, "This was only to the good." Only later did I come to understand what he had meant. Snow would cover our tracks and eliminate our scent which dogs could follow. It would dampen and disguise the sounds we might make and, above all, it would discourage the Germans from looking for us, and they would possibly assume that we would perish from exposure.

For many hours we walked steadily with only the shortest breaks. The guide led the column and spoke to no one except me, and then only in inarticulate grunts. In the beginning I made it a point to stay close to him, fearing he might attempt to slip away from us in an unguarded moment.

Two of the Poles took up the rear guard to keep the line together and help stragglers. The other Poles acted like sheepdogs, running up and down the column to maintain a constant liaison between front and rear. Their energy on the first day was enviable, though at times in their eagerness, and in spite of my full appreciation of their goodwill, they managed to irritate even me.

A persistent snow was falling and we were blinded by its dizzying flurries. I was soaked with perspiration from the effort of climbing and chilled to the bone by the cold air and whipping wind. All our energies were absorbed by the physical effort. We walked without thinking, grateful for every slight lull in the wind or the momentary thinning of the snowfall or a stretch of ground that was level and not too heavily covered with pebbles, which made walking in thin-soled city shoes painful and dangerous. My muscles ached and the rarefied cold air hurt my throat and lungs.

We were ill equipped for the weather and for mountain climbing. We did not have any of the provisions usually carried for such trips. We had no sugar, smoked bacon, or brandy, and we wore whatever clothes we had been wearing when we hastily left Paris. One of the Poles—he looked like an old man—wore a thin cloth suit. He had no overcoat and walked on felt slippers. I had had serious qualms about dragging him along in this condition. He spoke only Polish, but the other Poles had unanimously taken up his cause with such vehemence that I had left it at that.

The solid-looking Dutch contingent, used to flat country at sea level, were the first ones to tire, but exposed as we were on all sides it was too cold to rest for long.

Toward morning the guide brought us to an abandoned goatherd's summer shelter, which, hidden under a thick layer of snow, would have escaped our attention. Everyone collapsed in small heaps and, half in jest, half in real distress, pleaded for fire and food, fully aware that neither could possibly be provided. The guide warned us to put our shoes on again after warming our feet by massaging them briskly. He insisted we sleep with our shoes on despite the discomfort this caused, for our feet might swell and we would be unable to put our shoes back on the following night. He retired to one corner, curled up, and remained there, immobile like a hibernating animal. I was disappointed. I had hoped to be able to talk to him, to find out how much longer this trip would take.

I woke to an unaccustomed silence. I was uncomfortably wet and cold, though fairly well rested. With a start I remembered that the world was under snow. Huddled up around me lay my companions. Instinctively I checked the place where the guide was sleeping, but he was not there. I leaped up and ran to the door. There he stood in the snow looking at the sky. In the pale light of dusk the snow was gray.

A few men came out to look at the world. Their eyes were red, their faces creased by sleep, and they had several days' growth of beard. They took handfuls of snow and vigorously rubbed their hands and faces with it. We shook off the languor of sleep and readied to go off, wondering what lay ahead of us. The guide went back inside the hut and, from some hidden recess, produced a small burlap bag of chestnuts. Divided among us, it gave each three or four. Our fingers were cold and swollen and peeling the chestnuts proved to be a chore, but after the day's rest we were again full of drive and hope. We struggled and laughed, chewing the hard raw chestnuts with relish and delight.

After sleeping for a whole day in the heavy airless atmosphere of the goatherd's summer shelter, the cold air outside was invigorating. Once I was climbing again, I found out how painfully stiff were my muscles and how numb my feet.

There were no stars and the sky was opaque, promising more snow. The climbing became more difficult along long narrow gorges. The darkness and phosphorescent cover of snow altered my sense of perception and I stumbled over ill-defined or unseen obstacles. We passed a mountain spring cascading down a steep rock wall, a trickle among a frozen succession of icicles in which its water had become arrested in an intricate filigree pattern. We drank avidly and the icy water burned our lips and tongues. Our shirts, underwear, and outer clothes were wet and they bound and chafed. Our feet were blistered. I burned with fever and realized that for quite a while I had not taken the daily injection upon which I depended. The sealed glass phials, each containing a single day's dose, had frozen in their container and I did not dare use them anymore. I left the container behind, breaking yet another bond with the past. We chewed on our self-rationed chestnuts, making each mouthful last forever.

At the end of this night there was no shelter of any kind and we dug ourselves into the snow, huddling by twos and threes and fours—"Eskimo style," we said, not knowing or caring if Eskimos really did this. We were wet through and through, but by then we were somewhat conditioned to it and it bothered us less than the first day, though the hunger was worse. The altitude also affected me. I was more conscious of my breathing, which grew rapid. I felt strangely elated with an edge of lassitude. I felt very detached. Either I had stopped thinking or I simply did not care anymore. We felt a terrifying serenity which came from hunger, from being beyond the threshold of exhaustion, and from the rarefied mountain air.

Again we spent the day in a kind of suspended animation, but the following night it was more difficult than before to get up and shake off the fatalistic inertia. We moved only by night to avoid detection by German sharpshooters who, the guide told us, had been known to pick off fugitive climbers from hidden positions at great distances.

It had started to snow again, but at least the wind was practically still. As we stumbled on I thought I heard church bells ringing, not harmoniously as one imagined they would, but in an almost unpleasant counterpoint of metallic clanging. But when I strained to listen there was nothing but the rustle of my companions. A clear phrase arose in my otherwise blank consciousness: "at dusk in a strange land." Perhaps it was from a song heard long ago and now forgotten.

The Poles never tired of their self-imposed sheepdog run. I assumed it made them forget their own miseries. The guide was as taciturn as ever, uncomplaining, and he showed no sign of fatigue, hunger, or physical discomfort. Neither did he ever show concern with the suffering of the others. Maybe, like the Poles, this was his way of overcoming his preoccupations. It snowed more heavily and we had difficulty in keeping together for lack of visibility. The line stretched and turning back at one point I realized the man behind me had lost contact. I tried to overtake the one ahead, who was sometimes visible, sometimes not, to tell him to warn the others to halt and wait, or even to turn back, lest we become separated and lose one another. When we all huddled together again I saw through squinting eyes a group of strange survivors from some prehistoric period, with red swollen faces, their breath steaming, their beards matted with ice, their lips and facial skin cracked and blistered, bleeding. I tasted the vague taste of iron in the blood on my lips. Unconsciously they passed their swollen whitish tongues over their deformed lips, pulled up and showing their teeth. Their eyes were protectively half-closed against the snow and made them look like a different race, remnants of an Ice Age catastrophe.

The blizzard soon completely blinded and isolated us from our immediate surroundings. Holding on to one another, we edged our way toward a rock wall and desperately dug into a snowdrift piled high beneath an overhang. With my bare hands I dug in the soft snow and crept in the hole, pulling up my knees for warmth and protection. I tried to warm my stiff hands between my thighs, and then used my warmed hands to gently massage my nose, eyelids, and ears, all of which hurt from the cold. I pulled my knitted cap down over my eyes and mouth, but my breath moistened the wool before my lips and turned it to ice. Slowly I felt the cold creep into my feet, my calves, my knees, my lower back, my shoulders and neck, then the back of my head, while my thighs and belly held out and kept producing life-saving heat. A layer of powder-dry snow accumulated about and around us, integrating us with nature. Without extreme emotion, I imagined we would be found one day frozen in fetal positions like the Andean mummies. Though physically close, my companions and I were completely isolated from and indifferent to one another. We were like blind moles tunneling underground and going nowhere. There was no sound, no sight, and a slow process of paralysis was taking away the senses of touch, proportion, and relation.

I tried to think back. What had I done, or seen, or heard, where had I been, before I froze to death? Even this wildly unpredictable end was more peaceful than I could have speculated. For a while I wrestled with what to say to the others I had dragged along in this adventure, though I knew there was no more communication among us. In contrast to the hardening, insensitivity, and cooling of the outer crust of my body, the inside burned with fever and my thirst was unbearable. My tongue and throat were parched and it felt as if even my guts were dehydrated yet unexpectedly swollen from sucking on handfuls of packed snow we had been warned to leave alone. If you eat snow, the guide had said, you will go mad with thirst. Before the war I vaguely remembered reading melodramatic accounts of people who had perished in somewhat

similar circumstances and who left behind pathetic or flam-
boyant last messages.

I was brought out of my torpor by a repeated and violent
pain in the side, which continued until I emerged from the
abyss. The guide loomed over me. He was covered with snow
and he was persistently kicking me in the ribs to make me get
up. At that moment I hated him because I desperately wanted
to sleep and to forget.

Together we roused the others by kicking them as vigorously as before he had kicked me. I understood their resistance. All of them protested at first, with the single exception
of the flimsily dressed old Pole, who simply awoke from the
stir about him and who, to our surprise, was immediately
ready to proceed. Two or three resisted and pleaded, moving
their heads sideways in a disconsolate gesture of negation I
could never forget. Another rocked himself back and forth
and sobbed softly like a distressed infant. Nobody spoke; all
exchanges were by limited gestures and perhaps a few additional grunts. One of the Dutchmen stood up slowly only to
tumble over howling. The guide and the old Pole laid him out
and massaged his legs with snow, unmoved by his pleas to
leave him alone. Eventually we moved on again. It was still
daylight.

The landscape about us was blindingly white, rounded, and
gentle in shape. High drifts of snow had been sculpted by the
wind and looked like gigantic reclining female nudes. The air
was crisp and sounds seemed to carry with a predominance of
high tones almost to the elimination of lower ones.

It was unbelievably peaceful. The snow was two to three
feet deep and formed a smooth even rolling surface which,
however, did not correspond to the rock surface below. There
were treacherous snowdrifts four, five, and more feet deep,
indistinguishable from the rest of the field into which a man
could sink chest deep and from which he had to crawl out with
great difficulty. On the shady side of the mountain the snow
was a harsh white, but when it caught the rays of the setting
sun it was blinding and made the eyes smart. The snow
equally burned and froze us. Suddenly the sun set and it grew

colder. The surface of the snow had thawed slightly and through the night it hardened into an ice crust not strong enough to support our weight, so that we sank through it and its jagged edges cut and slashed our shins, knees, and thighs. In the lead the guide moved ahead with bared legs and with bleeding gashes criss-crossing his skin. For a while we tried to walk only in his steps, in the holes he had already made, but as we grew more tired we cared less and stumbled on as we could, leaving behind what amounted to a trench several feet deep by several feet wide. Several people suffered frostbite, but we kept moving on and on. I lost control of my coordination and felt my feet come down too hard and not in the positions I intended.

When our guide, hardened by experience and the lore of the mountain, kicked me back to life out of an autistic inertia, I fervently begged to let nobody awaken me ever again. But this was not to be; from then onward the only thing left for us to do was literally to struggle to our death.

My mind blurred and coherent thought was replaced by extravagant visionary experiences in which sense perceptions became scrambled; color and sound, taste and touch became interchangeable. Purples and reds became tangible and acquired gratifying taste and throbbing sound; blues fermented and greens tingled. Yet another part of me, very detached and clinical, wondered if this could be a snow counterpart of the mirages one sees in the desert sands.

Suddenly the guide made a raucous unhuman sound. He threw himself headlong on the snow and his whole body shook with dry sobs. He crept around on all fours and dug frantically in the snow with his hands. Instantly sobered, I caught up with him and saw him cross himself three times and afterward kiss his crossed thumb and index finger. He could not speak and I thought he had gone mad, never expecting this unexplained burst of emotion from him who throughout this adventure had shown himself controlled and dependable beyond words. He pointed and I saw a square iron obelisk protruding less than one foot above the snow, marking the border between France and Spain. Several thousand feet below us, framed between the Pass of Roncesvalles and the six-thousand-foot Pic d'Orhy, lay the watershed, and beyond that lay the gently leveling plains of Pamplona—Spain, and safety.

We plodded on for another long while, but now we were boosted by the hope of heat and food and safety. We found a small farmhouse with a huge overhanging roof typical of the region, buried under many feet of snow. As survivors of the blizzard we were welcomed with loud cheers. Most of our men simply let themselves collapse on the stone floor around the hearth. We were given boiled potatoes with lard, hot wine with cloves, bread, and garlic.

Before I relaxed completely and weakened my resolve, I decided to push on deeper into Spanish territory to inform the various Allied consular representatives of the arrival of some of their nationals. I had heard unpleasant rumors about fugitives who had been retrieved by the Germans from within Spanish territory or who had been forcibly returned to the Germans by the Spanish border police. When this became known, there had been some official investigation—inconclusive no doubt—but which had not returned to life those treacherously betrayed.

Unexpectedly, only the four Dutchmen were game enough to follow. I gave our guide all the French money I carried. After having more or less forced him into this adventure and after all he had done for us, I had to stop him from kissing my hands in gratitude. Then he left during the general commotion. He probably went on to another farm in the vicinity (in his condition he could not possibly have gone back) to avoid being arrested by the Spanish border police whenever they came to count and collect the new illegal arrivals.

The five of us limped through the snow on the road to the nearest hamlet. On the way we met a jovial rotund farmer sitting on a mule. He offered to lead us back and took us in charge. Because of my condition, he offered me a ride on his mule. As we neared the village we detected in the mountain air, besides the smell of woodfires, a slight odor of petrol and fried olive oil.

A narrow gorge of perhaps fifteen to twenty feet at most separated us from the sturdy stone houses squatting low under their great snow-covered overhanging roofs. A single tree trunk lay across this geological gap. A narrow stream of water below emphasized its depth and worked on our imaginations. The fat man led the way across it, but when he turned around to see if we were following he grinned jovially as he realized we were not his kind. He coaxed us to sit astride the tree and move ourselves forward in this seated position, but we were too tired to dare new adventures. Annoyed at our unreasonable childish behavior, he came back, but warned us that to walk around the cleft, instead of the six yards or so over the makeshift bridge, might mean several additional miles. Desolate about the added inconvenience, we felt we had no choice. Exhausted as we were, to attempt unaccustomed acrobatics could mean accidental death within reach of our goal. They walked on wearily while I sat awkwardly perched atop the mule. Unwilling to give in, and no doubt to prove a point, the man turned the mule around and engaged it, with me on top, onto the tree across the open space. It happened too unexpectedly for me to cry out, to slip off the beast, or to do anything else.

The mule moved along slowly but surefootedly. I froze immobile and held my breath for fear of fatally upsetting the animal's precarious balance. I stared straight ahead, avoiding at all cost looking sideways or downward. I broke out in profuse cold perspiration and thought for a moment I might faint from panic and vertigo. A sharp draft of cold air rose from the depth of the gorge. Through the body of the mule I could feel the scraping of its hoofs on the wood and the slightly tensed play of its muscles as it shifted its weight from one foot to the other. The mule reached the other side and, walking at a steady pace, took me into the village well ahead of the others. Helped by many hands I dismounted and once again was given a hero's welcome. At the local inn I was made to sit down at a table covered with a heavy blanket and underneath which burned charcoal in a brass *brasero*. I was surrounded by the local men as roasted mutton and brandy were forced on me. The owner of the mule soon joined us with my four Dutch companions. We were too tired to sleep; instead, and most carelessly in view of our long fast and exposure, we ate the rich fare and drank unguardedly as everyone competed in treating us, the heroes of the day.

CHAPTER FIFTEEN

We stayed in Orbaceite because the village was snowbound (or so we were told). Among us we possessed a fair number of gold pieces which we readily converted into *pesetas,* and our spending was extravagant. We asked to be allowed to telephone our respective embassies or consulates, but there was no communication possible. Then one day we were forced to tell the mayor that we were running out of money and asked him if he could arrange a loan for our subsistence until we could reach our national authorities to reimburse him or the locality. He left us somewhat hastily, after reassuring us that this would indeed present no problem. Instead we were unexpectedly surrounded by a number of Guardia Civil. Several held us under cover with their submachine guns while others handcuffed us. Miraculously the village was no longer snowbound. We were taken away in the back of an open truck. None of our earlier drinking and eating companions came to the rescue, which we did not and could not expect, but neither did they show themselves to bid us goodby. We spent a miserable night at the badly overcrowded jail in Pamplona. Arriving too late for the regular meal, we were obliged to buy bread at exorbitant blackmarket prices. The various guards begged for fountain pens or wristwatches, and even offered to trade for the shirts on our backs, our belts or suspenders. We were greatly bothered by fleas and for lack of pallets or blankets we dozed sitting up, taking turns at keeping watch over the others in our party.

The following day, after drinking the early morning chocolate made with boiling water, we were handcuffed again and

210

brought before *los juezes,* the judges, whoever they were or whatever judicial or administrative authority they represented. From there we were marched down the streets of Pamplona to the main railroad station. We boarded the passenger train still handcuffed and, after strenuously protesting, refused the Guardia Civil's attempt to make us pay for our own railroad tickets. We claimed we had no money, but we were never searched. On the crowded train the Guardia Civil agents removed the handcuffs from our wrists but chained up our ankles instead. The coach was crowded with peasants carrying bulky packages, baskets, crates, bags, and hens with their legs tied. The Guardia Civil were not unpleasant; I spoke to them in Spanish and at leisure investigated their unlikely three-cornered hats made of stiff black oilcloth with a black leather chinstrap. They wrapped themselves with dignity in their great theatrical capes. Past the train windows rushed the mountains of Navarre covered by somber oak forests, and then stark desolate landscapes. All we could do to pass the time was eat and drink what the people around us generously offered: *chorizo,* bread, raw onions, hard boiled eggs, lean smoked bacon and garlic, wine, and anís. The peasants spoke to us and showed us their sympathy in many ways, although one could sense they were intimidated by our police escort. These peasants helped render more indulgent our first impression and evaluation of Franco's Spain. We finally arrived at Miranda de Ebro, the infamous internment camp for foreigners between Burgos and Vitoria. The squalid white-washed barracks with their red-tiled roofs were neatly aligned and our first impression of the camp was favorable beyond expectations. It was, after all, the last station on the arduous road to Gibraltar or Lisbon and from there to London.

A triumphant sign over the entrance gate read TODO POR LA PATRIA. A loudspeaker blared out *paso dobles* sung in a metallic female voice accompanied by a somewhat frantic orchestra. The camp was surrounded by barbed wire and every 150 to 200 feet stood a shabbily dressed military guard. The sky overhead was blue and crowded with capricious little white clouds. The camp was situated between the river Ebro and the railroad tracks. In the distance we could see the mountains of Old Castile.

After having presented their receipts at the administration building and having them signed for delivery of the merchandise (us), the Guardia Civil removed our handcuffs and parted with an unanticipated display of affection and regret.

Everywhere prisoners with bare torsos sat on the ground in the sun, delousing shirts spread out over their outstretched legs. We were issued a metal military canteen, fork and spoon, a filthy blanket, and then assigned to one of the twenty-five numbered barracks. The *cabo* of my barracks was a Serbian and he appeared willing to help, after a fashion, and—he left no doubt about this—for a price.

The barracks was a huge hangar and the only permanent structures inside were balconylike concrete shells projecting on either side and running its full length. The upper levels were reached by three clumsy steps. Both lower and upper levels were less than six feet in height and had no outer walls. The prisoners had improvised makeshift partitions which, according to the camp's regulations, were illegal but which insured some privacy and kept in the heat. The separate cubicles were also heated illegally. These small low-ceilinged subdivisions were called *cals* by the old-timers and were shared by two or three people. A blanket served as a door. Making fire was forbidden, but every *cal* was equipped with a small woodburning stove ingeniously made out of a large tin can and connected by an incongruously improvised stovepipe protruding at a slant into the open inner space of the barracks. They whimsically evoked more menacing antitank guns in firing position, but filled the barracks with blinding, choking woodsmoke.

After having met my new companions and putting down my few belongings, I discreetly inquired about Gypsies in the camp. I was told there was one in the barracks of the "Internationals," but I was strongly advised against going there. It was a barracks in which the old-timers lived, the rough ones, those who had managed to survive The War (the Spanish

Civil War) and had seen their comrades perish either shot or
garotted to death by the Falangist victors—and, it was emphasized, they did not like transients.

I was invited to join the exclusive inner circle of our
barracks, which consisted mainly of professional pilots. Some
of them had flown Allied missions over Germany and had been
shot down, others had escaped from *Offlags*, POW camps for
officers. All were anxious to reach England. They were an
adventurous, extroverted, hard-drinking lot who before the
war had flown everywhere, tasted all manner of cooking, and,
to judge from their stories, possessed all kinds of women.
Since almost anything could be obtained in the camp of
Miranda de Ebro for money at the pilots' "officers' mess"—
which was just another *cal*—there was a profusion of Pedro
Domecq cognac, Negrita rum and Anís del Mono. The pilots
were both great drinkers and great talkers, and they talked of
Africa and the Sahara, of the Andes and South America, and
of the Far East.

The days in Miranda de Ebro started with an early morning
roll call at the Plaza Generalísimo Franco, the obligatory
presence at the raising of the Spanish colors, and unanimous
singing of the Spanish national anthem. I was told that at the
time there were forty-two nationalities represented among my
fellow prisoners.

Most of the camp was deep mud and the latrines were
housed in a barracks with a concrete floor full of holes, located
at the far end of the camp. They were, without doubt, the most
atrocious and offensively filthy installations of their kind I
ever saw, before or after and anywhere in the world. Using
these facilities—for which there was no alternative—was referred to as "going to visit Franco."

On the south side of the camp was the Promenade des
Anglais, after the famous promenade in Nice, where mostly
the transient and more privileged prisoners like ourselves
walked and talked. Miranda de Ebro also boasted an in-
firmary and a Catholic chapel where mass was said on Sun-
days, and a canteen that opened in the afternoon, where a
harsh, almost black Rioja wine was sold to those who could

afford it. There was a disaffected *calabozo,* a jail-within-the-camp affair. Occasionally a film was shown or lectures were organized by some of the more intellectual inmates. There also was a speakeasy-type bar run by a Bessarabian by the name of Berkowitz.

The polyglot cacophony of the camp was punctuated by the sentries' long-drawn cries of *"Alerta,"* repeated like cries of distress at irregular intervals through night and day, and the equally monotonously repeated *"Se vende pan"*—Bread for sale, or *"Se vende . . ."* whatever was being hawked at that moment. Everything was for sale

Besides the vexation of mud and the ever-present stinging woodsmoke from the illegal indoor fires, there was abundant vermin of all kinds and varieties with which to contend, as well as the debilitating gastrointestinal affliction simply known locally as Miranditis.

The camp had an inordinate number of stray dogs who had adopted certain barracks and their inhabitants as their own.

The semisolid, semisoup camp food was called *roncho.* On top of it floated a layer of orange and badly refined olive oil. It consisted mainly of cabbage and various beans, occasionally some rice, and floating lumps of unidentifiable meat, bones, and bits of skin. The prisoners traditionally gulped down the *roncho* standing up, possibly to be near the cauldrons in case there was some left over for a second half-helping on the basis of first come, first served.

I went to see the Gypsy at Barracks 24 and met the man who called himself Lolya Menjain. We spoke in Romanes and, to the wonderment of all the other Internationals, within minutes all barriers between us were down. Lolya knew Pulika and had for a short time lived and traveled with our *kumpania* in 1936 or thereabouts, when he had come to Spain from Odessa. He had been sheltered and helped out in various ways by the Lowara and expressed his gratitude to them. He knew many of the Rom with whom I had grown up and slowly the image emerged in my memory of a young Russian Kalderash who had stayed with us. This man called Lolya before me, however, was to all appearances an old man, until he convinced me of what years in captivity had done to him.

As Gypsies were wont to do when they met, we talked only about Gypsy tribal affairs, to the exclusion of the life, world, regulations, and affairs of the Gaje. It was considered rude among Gypsies to question other Rom about the *modus vivendi* they had managed to evolve or the practical arrangements which led to this state. The priority of the first Gypsy on the spot was accepted and, if he so willed, he offered the newcomer protection and advice. In Gypsy fashion, Lolya introduced me to the other old timers as his cousin. They accepted me as such and I became a frequent visitor to Barracks 24. Lolya told me that several other Rom, calling themselves Greeks from Odessa, the Cristos, had recently been released from Miranda and that when I left he would send me to them. The broken chain was relinking itself.

The Internationals represented the hard core of the camp and they were its undisputed rulers, even though this was not at first apparent. They or their protégés held all key posts from communal kitchen on down and the *cabos* paid them tribute. The ruling *cal* was dominated by a strange troika. First was the clean-shaven energetic Roosevelt—no known first name—who always wore a short black-leather jacket. He implied he was a Texan, but spoke no English and had been a political commissar during the war. His sinister sidekick was known either as *el cojo,* the one with the limp, or as *el Italiano,* though he spoke only Spanish and that with a pronounced Andalusian verve and piquancy. He was said to be the local "enforcer" who saw to it that the underground's edicts were carried out and who intimidated and took care of informers and recalcitrant elements. The third one was my newly adopted "cousin," who I strongly suspected had no political affiliations and no particular ambitions, but managed to maintain his position in the triumvirate by unadulterated Gypsy bluff.

There were Yugoslavs, Rumanians, Hungarians, and even some Germans, survivors of the *Thaelmann Kolonne,* anti-Nazi volunteers who had fought on the Loyalists' side. In the evening when they drank the harsh Rioja wine they still occasionally sang forbidden songs like:

> *Wir, im ferne Vaterland geboren,*
> *Nahmen nichts als Hass im Herzen mit.*
> *Doch wir haben die Heimat nicht verloren*
> *Unser Heimat ist heute vor Madrid.*

> Born in a faraway fatherland
> We took with us nothing but our hate.
> Still we have not lost our homeland,
> For our homeland today is here, before Madrid.

Many of the other Internationals claimed Central and South American nationalities in order to be spared from the death penalty that otherwise might have been imposed by Franco's police, though most of these were in fact Spanish born and bred. There were no Mexicans or Russians. There were a few Dutch anarchists, but they refused all contact with the more recent arrivals from Holland. There was also a pathetic punch-drunk Cuban Negro, a silent part-Indian from Santo Domingo, and a lone Chinese. They were bitter against a world that had chosen to forget them, and the years of misery, betrayal, and captivity had made them misfits in the new world shaping around them. Like the rest of Spain outside the barbed wire, they had taken to saying *mañana,* which is best translated as "some day" rather than "tomorrow," which it never meant.

Yet, for me, "some day" came and I was released from the camp—some said liberated and others called it dismissed—through the diplomatic intercession, as I was told later, of Lord Ponsonby and Anthony Eden. For Lolya I left behind all I possessed. I went to Madrid by overnight train; once again, from living in conditions worse than cattle I passed without transition to first-class sleeper coach.

I stayed in Madrid at an excellent hotel while my Belgian passport was made ready. I felt impressed and unfamiliar with the idea of waiting for a real passport, with my own name and particulars, and suddenly I knew the transition would not be easy. From long exposure I had acquired a set of semiautomatic reflexes: "right ones" could become "wrong ones."

I suddenly longed to see my parents in England and my little sister and people, just plain, regular, free people; not specialists, neither victims, nor agents, nor types, nor characters nor ex-anythings. Yet I was also afraid to find out what I had become during those years. I was fitted for tailormade suits and overcoat, and since the money was allotted by the government I bought all those things a young man of good family background needed. I was forced to report to police headquarters at the Puerta del Sol. I lived in an unreal world to which I felt no affinity and in which I felt I was an interloper. The rare contacts I had with security officers of the Allied missions were equally unpleasant, as I was aware of mutual distrust and only willful understanding. They were the textbook boys while I had been there. However I easily adjusted to the rhythm of life in Spain. I did not mind the late dinner hour, the formality in dress and attitude. I like the natural dignity of the people, though I found the elegant life in sharp discomforting contrast to the innumerable crippled and blind beggars everywhere.

When I could no longer restrain myself, I went like a haunted soul in search of the Gypsies. I asked about and searched the popular sections of Madrid, with their noisy lively crowds and the smells of fried codfish and saffron, of olive oil, garlic, and urinals. My inquiries led me to a working-class section near the Puente de Vallecas with monotonous rows of low, gaunt, untidy-looking houses and an occasional clump of dusty palms. Old women sat on their doorsteps. They were draped in black and looked as fierce and severe as the younger women, occasionally visible inside the shadowy interiors, looked provocative. On a plaza near the public baths were a crowd of ragged barefoot boys, intensely purposeful little bootblacks. Everywhere donkeys and mules were used for transportation. I asked where I could find *los Gitanos,* the Spanish designation for Gypsies, until I was led to a remote dirt road. There was a row of lime-washed shacks and in front of these milled about a lively group of boys and young women in an extravagant array of colorful clothes. They stood in sharp contrast to the surrounding Spanish working-class of the *barrio*.

But even from a distance I could tell they were not Rom. These people at first seemed like a theatrical version of the nomadic Rom I was used to. Unlike the Rom, who would at least have feigned indifference, they watched me approach with undisguised eagerness, like performers awaiting the applause they considered their due. I greeted them in Romanes but they did not understand me. Before they spoke to me in Spanish to find out what I wanted, they talked among themselves in a language I could not follow. When I told them I was looking for Gitanos they said that was what they were. When I explained I was looking for another kind of Gypsies, for the Rom, they exclaimed with sudden insight, "You must be looking for *los Húngaros*. They are not Gypsies, they are Hungarians." And their whole attitude changed. I was invited to sit down and there followed an excited deliberation in Gitano language. From inside the houses people came to look at me with a mixture of curiosity, commiseration and also a touch of condescension I failed to understand. I explained I had been released from the internment camp of Mirando de Ebro and that before that I had escaped from the Germans and crossed the mountains. They offered me food, drink, and even a small amount of money to help me out. They asked many questions and what I replied was repeated to others and passed along all over the lot.

Several older men and women were fetched to talk to me. The young men seated on chairs in the shade resumed playing the guitar and the young girls went back to practicing intricate dancing steps. They snapped their fingers and assumed fierce expressions. They held their arms over their heads momentarily poised in a gesture of threat. Remaining on one spot, they stamped the floor in furious staccato. Their dance partner, a young man in well-cut, high-waisted, tight-fitting trousers, revealing an exaggerated male camber, strutted about like some haughty peacock. His face was gaunt and very dark and he moved as in a trance. In his obsessive masculinity he reminded me of a tomcat in heat. The girl, who obviously was the star of the *cuadro* (group), was immodestly called Terremoto, earthquake. They took rapid turns at performing and seemed polished professionals.

The older men took me to a nearby wineshop where we toasted each other with *manzanilla* and ate endless *tapas,* those bite-sized hors d'oeuvres consisting of fried shrimp, pork, beef, sardines, squid, eggs, olives, and chickpeas, *ad infinitum.* Through a break in the buildings I could see in the distance the arid sierras and the barren plateaus surrounding the city, insinuating in the capital city of Spain a consciousness of the countryside. The Gitanos—or, as they referred to themselves, the *Cale,* our Romani word for black—promised to take me to the Húngaros that night, but they insisted on first showing me, the stray one, the hospitality of their race. Since we were forced for lack of another common language to speak Spanish together, the other patrons could follow our conversation and it was transparent enough from my appearance that, though in full command of the language, I was an alien to Spain. Slowly the conversation drifted to bullfighting, though we were off season, and from bullfighting in general to Manolete, the tall, gaunt, revered hero of the Fiesta Brava. His posters were everywhere. (He was to die in the arena of Linares a few years later in his early thirties.) They talked about his refusal to compromise and of what they called his tauromachian purity. And they admired the qualities of the bulls with almost equal partiality.

Late that evening I arrived, accompanied by my erstwhile Cale hosts, at a large camp of tents off a dirt road. Dogs barked in the night, joined by the wild unearthly sound of a donkey braying. The Gitanos yelled above the din in Spanish. Several men emerged from a nearby tent, silenced the dogs with some difficulty, and came toward us. They were Rom. A sigh rose from deep inside of me, or maybe it was a long-restrained sob. I had difficulty controlling my voice. While I was made to feel welcome, the Gitanos were not invited in, and after my thanking them they said good night and left.

The night sky overhead was clear and full of stars. The air was cold and crisp and had the peculiar tang which came from burning charcoal. Around us all was quiet now. In the otherwise silent houses of the Gaje an infant wailed.

Unlike the Cale, the Rom were fleshy and they stood and moved with a slow and dignified ease. One was called Djordji and the younger one Hanzi. They were the sons of Tshompi, who had a legendary reputation among the Rom everywhere. The third one was but a boy. We lingered for a few minutes outside the tent and talked. The tents seemed huge in front of me in the dark and I could hear the voices inside. Tshompi came out. He was a tall erect old man with powerful shoulders, perhaps seventy-five or eighty years old. He had wide-set eyes, a hawk's nose, and a very strange smile. I repeated to him that I came from abroad and that I was a Lowari. *"Devlesa avilan,"* he said. "You came with God. You are among your own." He lifted the tarpaulin that closed the entrance and I stepped inside the huge tent, which was only lit by the glow of the charcoal-burning *brasero.* Two women crouched silently fanning the embers. One was old, tall, and white-haired. She was Liza, Tshompi's wife and of Lowari stock. There were several other Rom visiting Tshompi. I was glad it was dark and I hoped they would not notice how deeply I was moved. I drank the Turkish coffee they offered me and ate the *makoski reteshska,* the moonseed strudel they set before me. Liza was distantly related to Pulika. She told me that her daughter-in-law Borinka, only recently married to their son Hanzi, was the daughter of Notarka. I knew him and his two brothers, Pali and Mutshoro.

Suddenly my whole life with Pulika and his *kumpania* and all the things I had been part of, and which had seemed to recede and fall into perspective, rushed back upon me more vivid even than before, when they still could be touched. Tshompi, sensing my disarray, gave me brandy and for a while we drank silently in the dark. Then they turned to small talk about local events and gossip. But before long the conversation turned back to my relatives, the Lowara. At first they talked about those who had left Spain recently to go to Central and South America. They said I might want to join Loiza la Vakako who, with his extended family, had recently gone to Brazil. They talked about Tshompi's youngest son Bebi, who had left for Guatemala and Honduras. Then they asked me about old Tshurka, who was married to Baba. They had last been heard of from Holland. They were known to possess Nicaraguan passports and could conceivably have managed to escape in time. I told them I had heard they had been arrested as enemy aliens when Nicaragua had declared war on Germany alongside the United States, but as far as I knew they were safe, having escaped the fate of other Gypsies.

As was inevitable, the conversation returned to the persecutions of the Rom under the Nazis, and I forced myself to tell what I knew both from hearsay and from what I had personally lived through. "We have heard," said Tshompi, silently pouring a libation to the dead and the dying from his cup of Pedro Domecq brandy onto the rug-covered earthen floor. For a long time afterward I was unable to utter a sound and I cursed what I suddenly came to see as my own undeserved survival. I spent the rest of the night among the Rom, as in a thousand dreams I had wanted to do. As I dozed off into half-sleep I imagined I heard the neighing of horses and the squeaking of wagon wheels. That night, after a long time, I dreamed again of the Lowara: ever wandering, separating, reuniting.

The following day started with the usual sweet black Turkish coffee. We nibbled some tiny wild strawberries brought in by a Gajo neighbor. Hanzi had awakened me and it was as if we had always known each other. Outside the tent we poured water for each other to wash from a brass pitcher of vaguely Moorish design. After this we went with a few other young Gypsy men to a nearby place to drink anís. Later on for breakfast we had the leftovers from the previous night's meal: yellow rice with chicken, Spanish sausage, seafood, and lobster. Liza commented to me about it not being a very

Lowari kind of morning meal. Only shortly afterward old Tshompi asked me, very concerned, "How long ago is it since you have last eaten?" I knew he meant by that how long ago it had been since I had eaten among the Rom, rather than among strangers. Since it had been many months, Tshompi exclaimed, "Only now I realize how hungry you must be! How thoughtless of me not to have asked this sooner!"

That day I wandered aimlessly about between the huge dark canvas tents on the piece of wasteland. Several times I went to the nearby *bodega* wineshop, whenever Gypsy men I had not met before came and invited me there, as was the custom. I went along with Hanzi on some errands and somewhat listlessly explored a few of the narrow alleys in the immediate vicinity of the encampment. The Rom seemed to be on very good terms with their Spanish neighbors and there was a certain amount of visiting back and forth between them, a thing I had not known in my earlier experiences with the Rom. Tshompi's group practiced retinning and coppersmithing on a large scale. All day long Rom from other groups came and went. Most of them identified themselves as *Grekura,* Greeks. I also noticed that the women rarely told fortunes. Though they themselves said they were Greeks, their Spanish acquaintances addressed them as Húngaros. Later I learned this was the generic term used to differentiate between them and the Gitanos, who were considered Spain's own Gypsies, as opposed to the "foreign" ones. The Spanish neighbors seemed to subsist on bare necessities in a static, though proud and dignified, poverty. Yet they had *alegría,* that uniquely Spanish capacity for being happy, neither fatalistically accepting fate nor needlessly bemoaning it. In contrast to them, the Rom lived in ease and comfort.

That night when I came back to Tshompi's tent many Rom had gathered there and I found an abundant and festive meal had been prepared—in my honor. "To sate your hunger," the old man said. "And through you I want this also to be in homage—to the others. *Te avel angla lende.*" This was a barely disguised formula used at the beginning of the *Pomana,* the feast for the dead. Whenever a Rom died, a lavish feast was offered after the burial, nine days, six weeks, six months, and one year after the death. These feasts marked the end of particular periods during which certain restrictions of mourning, determined by the degree of kinship, were renounced. No one was permitted to mourn beyond one year. Life must go on. And as important as it was considered to be for the peace of the dead soul to be made aware of the affection and loyalty of those left behind, it was equally important that we should not sorrow exceedingly. As the Rom wisely put it, "The mourned should be allowed to continue on his voyage in the new life, as we should resume our lives." The Rom said on these occasions, *"Putrav lesko drom angla leste, te ne inkrav les mai but palpale mura brigasa"*—I open his way into the new life and release him from the fetters of my sorrow. The Rom knew that stagnant water grew foul and that, like water, life must flow.

Tshompi and the other Rom were affectionate and tactful; it was difficult to remember that barely twenty-four hours earlier I had not known any of them. They ate and drank, and Djordji and Hanzi, and occasionally Tshompi himself, took turns picking out special morsels and feeding me with them. They repeatedly toasted my health. They drank and in this way forced me to drink, not, as they said, in order for me to forget, but in order for me to remember. They embraced me and each new gesture of tenderness, by perverse contrast, aroused in me specters of the past, of Pulika and my immediate family. And the Rom knew this. I cried openly for them who, with an equal claim to life, had been destroyed because they were considered a threat to the Third Reich, and perhaps also because they believed in the possibilities of freedom.

I drank with Tshompi and his guests and at their request I sang *brigaki djilia,* the epic songs of sorrow. In turn they took up the refrain and joined in "carrying" the song. I was still in poor health due to my wartime experiences and I knew I was becoming intoxicated, but the Rom urged me on. Tshompi insisted I drink with him from his glass, and I could not refuse. I felt a feverish drowsiness invade me, alternating with hot flashes of anxiety, like stabbings. I needed fresh cold air.

Hanzi, attentive to my needs, went outside of the tent with me. We walked. The skies were darkening and the evening was quiet. The parched barren nakedness of the distant Castilian landscape was veiled by dusk.

The drinking and singing of sad songs went on until the birds noisily started to greet the dawn. Aware of being surrounded by the strong and undemanding love of the Rom, and in an unwilled ecstasy of disorientation, I sensed a breakthrough, a slow emergence from all that had been. I was still amenable to healing. I now lived with Tshompi's *kumpania*. Step by step I could again become a human being in the community of men.

With melancholy, I thought I heard Pulika say to me, "One day you will learn again to open the closed fist. Only life makes sense."